This book is to be returned on
or before the date stamped below

17. JUL 1999   ~~CANCELLED~~

− 6 MAR 2000

27 MAR 2000

− 4 MAY 2000

− 8 JUN 2000

UNIVERSITY OF PLYMOUTH

PLYMOUTH LIBRARY

Tel: (01752) 232323
This book is subject to recall if required by another reader
Books may be renewed by phone
CHARGES WILL BE MADE FOR OVERDUE BOOKS

Ext. 219

A book may be renewed by telephone or by personal visit
if it is not required by another reader.
CHARGES WILL BE MADE FOR OVERDUE BOOKS

THE MANAGEMENT OF WATER RESOURCES
IN ENGLAND AND WALES

The Management of Water Resources in England and Wales

A seminar organised by LORD ZUCKERMAN
Edited by B.M. FUNNELL and R.D. HEY
With an introduction by SIR NORMAN ROWNTREE

SAXON HOUSE | LEXINGTON BOOKS

Published by

SAXON HOUSE, D. C. Heath Ltd.
Westmead, Farnborough, Hants., England.

Jointly with

LEXINGTON BOOKS, D. C. Heath & Co.
Lexington, Mass. USA.

ISBN 0 347 01062 8
Library of Congress Catalog Card Number 74-12658
Printed in Great Britain
by Unwin Brothers Limited
The Gresham Press, Old Woking, Surrey
A member of the Staples Printing Group

Contents

List of figures

List of tables

Preface

In the Spring of 1973 a new Water Bill was introduced into the British Parliament containing far-reaching proposals for the management of water in England and Wales. From 3–4 March 1973, during the passage of the Bill through Parliament, a seminar was held at the University of East Anglia to discuss the implications of the impending legislation both for the water industry and the public at large. This was attended by many distinguished representatives of British water management and industry. The Water Act, based on this Bill with some amendments, was subsequently enacted and a re-organised management structure based on the Act introduced on 1 April 1974.

The seminar was one of a series on environmental problems made possible by a generous grant from the Ford Foundation.

The transcript of the discussion was prepared by Mr. L. W. Bear.

Introduction

Sir NORMAN ROWNTREE

There is a lot to be said for knowing why it is appropriate to hold a seminar like this, why Parliament is at this moment discussing water management, and why throughout the world countries are taking the subject seriously. This morning the water industry seems to be fairly good: the tap works, the sewage disappears, and if one wants to go fishing one can get it somewhere. So why is everyone worried?

I must go back to the Industrial Revolution. There was a famous Act, the Water Works Clauses Act, 1847, which set the pattern of water supply in this country for ninety-eight years — a remarkable piece of legislation. It was based on the needs of the cities, the need for purity of water without knowing how and why water carried disease, and as a result people went to the hills, stored water, carried it safely away in pipes, and it did not appear again until the tap was opened in the city. After the war the Water Act of 1945 introduced minor controls, but its main objective was to improve administration. I do not think that Act was as good as the 1847 one.

After 1945, when public water supply was the main interest, effluent disposal still continued in the traditional way. The scientific side was quite good. Biological treatment was carried out but it was done on a parochial basis as it is now. Each community wants to get rid of its sewage and not see it again; the fact that somebody else sees it afterwards is not of interest to the authority disposing of it.

In the 1950s some of us found that in order to get adequate water supplies in some parts of the country, particularly the Merseyside—Cheshire area, it was no longer possible to rely on piping water from the hills or taking water directly out of the nearest river or out of the ground. Something more was needed so we reverted to the way in which water had traditionally been managed before the Industrial Revolution, i.e. storing the water, releasing it to run down the rivers and taking it out as and when wanted, perhaps re-using it many times on the way. This policy started on the River Dee, because the Dee River Board wanted to control flooding by storing water in Bala lake. At the same time a number of water undertakings wanted large quantities of water. In particular the West Cheshire Water Board wanted to increase its supply by 200 per cent in two or three years. That is the sort of situation which makes theoretical discussion of water demand a subject of some cynicism to the water undertakings, when one industry can come along and completely disrupt ultimate predictions in that way.

There were, however, problems. An industry could come and settle itself halfway along the river under the old Common Law provisions and take the water out without paying for it. An industry could also put sewage back in and make the water unusable. New legislation was needed, and this and other developments led to the 1963 Act, which represented a complete change in regard to the country's water management. The old Common Law provisions had to go, and a licensing system was introduced so that people could not interrupt the proper management of the river. Unfortunately the 1963 Act was primarily aimed at the urgent problem of the time — the quantity of water that had to be made available — and it had practically no regard to quality, that problem having been thought to be resolved by the Pollution Act of 1961. Since 1963 we have had this new organisation of river authorities. Britain and France were the first countries in the world to do this comprehensively; France did it because of pollution and we did it because we wanted to make adequate quantities of water available.

In the process of this revolution we discovered that we had only gone halfway and that the quantity of water available was dependent on the quality of the water. We are now in a situation where there has to be complete integration of water management not just for supplying water in taps but for creating satisfactory and healthy conditions in the river and for enabling industry to choose where it wants to go, because water is not the deciding factor from an economic point of view, in the location of industry: labour, sources of materials, and markets determine location. So the new system is looking at overall management for England and Wales as a whole. It has highlighted the problem of pollution management. The re-use of water which already happens on a very large scale will increase that problem rapidly unless new concepts of pollution management come in.

1   Water Needs and Resources

B. RYDZ

The opening session of this seminar has the all-embracing title of 'needs and resources'. Although this can only be a sketchy introduction to this theme I hope to convey something of the interdependence of needs and resources in a country like this, where water quality management, changes in water re-use policy, and decisions on industrial location can in effect produce new resources. For instance, to site a new power station downstream of a major sewage effluent outfall may turn the latter into a valuable resource.

We use water as an agent for many purposes but usually as a work-horse for the carriage of heat or materials. It scarcely ever undergoes a chemical change and in this country very little of it even suffers a change of state at our hands. If we think of it as a vehicle, rather than as a commodity, it is easier to remember the convoluted cycle of uses and re-uses in which it can take part, and to appreciate that simple comparisons of the amounts needed with the output of sources play only a limited role in analysis of the water resource problem.

By far the largest quantities of water are used to condense steam at power stations — in effect, to carry away the heat which we cannot convert into power. At the other extreme we boil water on the domestic cooker to carry heat into foodstuffs. In between we use water on various scales to carry raw materials and wastes into and out of our bodies as well as into and out of our factories.

If we added up all these jobs and never used the same water twice before it returned to the sea we should probably find that we use nearly 150 million cubic metres each day (m^3/d) in England and Wales. More than 140 million m^3/d of this is used in power stations and industrial plants, 90 per cent of it for cooling. But some 50 million m^3/d of the cooling water used is sea or estuary water and another 60 million m^3/d is fresh water, passing round cooling circuits, from which the heat is removed by evaporation. Only 2 per cent to 4 per cent of this 60 million m^3/d has to be provided in new make-up water to these circuits. Consequently the amount of fresh water taken into homes and factories for all purposes in 1971 was only about 42 million m^3/d. Of this about 14 million m^3/d was supplied by public water undertakings, about a third of it to industrial users.

It may be thought that the use of saline water and water in evaporative circuits is not relevant to problems of fresh water resources. Its relevance lies, however, in the opportunities for substituting one kind of cooling for another, either by the choice of coastal instead of inland sites, especially for power stations, or by introducing more evaporative circuits, with cooling towers etc., in lieu of once-through cooling arrangements.

Even the 42 million m^3/d abstracted from sources, however, cannot be regarded as an effective call on water resources since much of it is used successively by neighbouring riparian users. In some cases after going through the home and the sewage works it becomes available in the river for industrial abstraction, in certain areas, for abstraction to feed another public water supply. It is not easy to define any net total demand on resources as a result of this pattern of uses. However, if we allow for the in situ needs of rivers, at the river mouth and elsewhere, we can assess the capacity of each river system to bear extra burdens — greater losses of water or increased inputs of waste; its need for additional resources; increased inflows of water or improved water treatment plants. Each such assessment, however, is specific to the pattern of uses and the in situ flow and quality targets which we envisage; it can be changed, for instance, by changing the relative locations of intakes and outfalls along a river course.

On the resources side, it is estimated that we dispose of between 190 and 200 million cubic metres of run-off per average day over the whole of England and Wales, an amount of the same order of magnitude as that of the total of water uses given above. But, as with the latter, the relevant amount for our purposes is much smaller because of variation in distribution in both time and space. The lowest flow would be zero were it not for storage in aquifers, soils, lakes and rivers.

The lowest dry-weather flow with which we usually concern ourselves in water resource management — an event occurring perhaps once in fifty years — is maintained by natural storage at between 5 per cent and 20 per cent of the average run-off; say, 10 per cent or 20 million m^3/d for England and Wales as a whole. By providing storage in reservoirs of between 1,500 and 2,000 million m^3/d man has probably raised this dry-weather flow in total by something like 12 million m^3/d. By providing perhaps another 2,000 million m^3 of surface storage, as well as improving the use of some of the storage we already have and using nature's underground storage to better advantage, we could raise the dry-weather output to between 45 and 50 million m^3/d, or about a quarter of the mean flow. It is to this level of provision that the strategic plans of the Water Resources Board relate. Such plans may make ends meet until the end of the century or, on the reduced population estimates now being

2

made, perhaps for a decade thereafter.

By that time the total of water uses will probably have expanded very greatly — to an extent that we have not yet found it either possible or necessary to estimate. But we have reason to believe that expansion of the public water supply system to about double its present output — say, to 28 million m^3/d — will provide a sufficient basis for the necessary growth in industrial water use. It will provide the basis in that new storage is being proposed almost wholly to meet this expansion of public supply; and in that successive re-use of the resulting sewage effluents together with intensified re-use within industry — especially by increased resort to recirculatory cooling — is being relied upon to meet almost all growth in industrial use from private sources.

Such an outcome will depend, of course, on industries being in the right places relative to dischargers of effluent or, alternatively, on the use of distribution systems to get river-grade water to where it is wanted. It will also depend upon increased investment in effluent treatment since waste loads, like waste heat loads, are likely to increase much faster than the modest augmentation of dry-weather flows proposed from new storage reservoirs. Of course, an attempt to manage such an expansion of use on an even more slender basis of new storage resources ('primary resources') would further intensify the problems of water quality control, and vice versa.

The system which has been envisaged in plans made by the Water Resources Board is one in which the rivers of England and Wales are interlinked, by aqueduct where necessary, and the whole system is provided with an optimised pattern of storage points. These will of necessity mainly be in the wetter areas of the north and west where more economic storage sites exist, and where storage provides a better return in yield.

A selection has been made from indentified storage capacity sufficient to meet about four times the estimated needs of the next thirty years. The opportunities identified include:

(a) simple improvements in the use made of existing storage (e.g. conversion of a compensation reservoir to methodical river regulation);
(b) generation of extra storage underground by intermittent pumping for river regulation;
(c) increased storage on existing sites for which several opportunities exist in Wales; and
(d) new storage sites, both inland and in estuaries.

The preference has been to deploy them in this order; that is to say, to resort first to those schemes which are least expensive in capital and which are likely to interfere least with existing interests and uses of land.

The pressures which are brought to bear on plans for water resource development are well known to all of us, and it is these which have helped to shape alternative system options and to guide the Board in the choices on which their recommendations will be based.

Some major new surface storage sources are needed urgently — especially those at Kielder (Northumbria), Brenig (Dee and Clwyd), Carsington (Trent) and Craig Goch (Wye) — and for these option of estuary storage is not open. The project for expansion of the existing reservoir at Craig Goch in particular is a key one which can sustain growing water use in the West Midlands and South Wales for a long period as well as helping out the Thames and the Dee and Clwyd areas for about a decade. The use of the Craig Goch reservoir in this way will necessitate the development of tunnel links from Wye to Severn and from Severn to Thames, bringing to fruition, but in a different form, a project, first mooted over a century ago, for the supply of the metropolis from central Wales. Aqueducts from Wye to Usk and from Severn to Dee would also be needed. Kielder reservoir, which would regulate the North Tyne, is likewise intended to serve the other main rivers of Northumbria, and perhaps Yorkshire and Lincolnshire, through link tunnels.

Over the longer term the Board is likely to recommend some estuary development, probably in the Dee, but not to advocate simultaneous development in a number of estuaries. Groundwater development and the re-development of existing reservoir sites will continue to play a part where opportunities exist.

A plan which seeks to optimise the pattern of development over England and Wales as a whole necessarily puts considerable strain on any system of independent authorities, whether twenty-nine or ten in number, unless they are provided with a forum in which they can commit themselves to a strategic framework and evolve machinery for operating and financing it effectively. This is no simple matter since, for instance, it is of the essence that inter-regional transfer systems be operated intermittently to match weather conditions and in combination with indigenous storage facilities in each region.

The Board's plans have of course been evolved in co-operation with authorities in the field although the responsibility for the recommendations in their forthcoming report will be that of the Board. The recommendations are likely to include only nine or ten substantial new surface storage schemes, about half of them on existing reservoir sites, to meet the needs of most of the country for the next thirty to forty years, together with groundwater management projects which are expected to provide about a quarter of the growth in output. There are some possible developments, such as the filling of underground storage in the London Basin by recharge, and the abstraction of water from the River Trent for potable supplies, on which it would be premature to make a judgement. The latter, of course, exemplifies the basic choice of the balance between re-use and new storage on which water resource strategy ultimately turns.

Forward planning, and indeed the storage—transmission strategy which I have outlined, depend upon a fabric of judgements about the likely levels of achievement by given dates in various new fields, such as ground-water storage management, run-off prediction for economical river regulation, management of complex reservoir and inter-basin transfer systems and so on. This requires a level of understanding, more subtle and demanding than any customer—contractor relationship, with persons familiar with research in those fields. It will cease to carry conviction unless such an understanding can be maintained in any future organisation.

Likewise the evolution of relevant strategic plans and options demands a continuous feedback of judgement from people concerned with policy recommendations; not a feedback angled to steer the planners towards any particular set of conclusions but one designed to make their necessarily limited range of optional packages suitable to satisfy the people for whom the work is ultimately being done.

The particular strength of the Water Resources Board's approach, I believe, has been in the maintenance of links in one small organisation between 'planning', research, and the drafting of broad advice on policy. It would be a mistake, I think, to assume that the same service could be rendered by planners lacking these stimuli.

The Board's proposals for a co-ordinated storage network will provide about 10 million m^3/d of the 12 million m^3/d of increased dry-weather flow which is referred to above; the remainder will be provided in various projects of a more local character. The use of comparatively few large storage projects maximises flexibility of allocation. Because such an inter-linked system is less at the mercy of local weather conditions as well as of unexpected changes in local demand it should be able to function with less surplus capacity, on average, than a system of smaller sources each linked to one demand centre, without loss of reliability. Allowing for this, its cost will be no greater.

The first generation of schemes referred to above is required to meet needs which are expected to arise in the second half of this decade. It now seems likely that in at least some areas there will be one or two anxious years before these projects come into service. These schemes should suffice, save in a few localities, to meet needs until 1990 or later so that decisions on the timing of the next generation of schemes are generally not due until nearly ten years from now. It is towards that time that the rate of growth of demand will have to be re-examined. Over the period during which these plans have been evolved (1965–73) the expectation of population growth in England and Wales to the year 2001 has fallen from over seventeen million persons to less than seven million, and it will not be surprising if further substantial changes in estimate occur. For the time being it has been necessary to examine the alternative strategies against various scenarios of future demand growth, etc., so as to be satisfied that their ranking in terms of cost is unlikely to change.

I hope that the Board's preferred long-term strategy will be widely considered and debated when it is published, and that it will receive a measure of endorsement, with or without changes, as a point of departure for future detailed planning. I feel sure that future proposals, both strategic and local, can be evaluated better in the context of such a general strategy. The adoption of a strategy, its progressive modification and the agreement of operating arrangements should be functions of the Regional Water Authorities through their central body, the National Water Council.

Any water conservation plan is an attempt to make some sort of equation between needs and resources. In the short time at my disposal I have embraced this theme only in the most general way, but I do hope to leave some impression of the relative magnitude of our needs and our resources and at the same time to emphasise that we are not concerned with a simple equation between them, as is the case with many consumable commodities, but with describing a complicated pattern of repeated uses, and envisaging some plausible pattern of use and re-use, with an appropriate primary resource base, for the future.

We know more about some parts of this pattern than others, and analysts and planners are always tempted to concern themselves with the respectable pieces about which they have evolved some theory and to brush the rest under the carpet. Much more thought has been given to refining assessments of the probability of failure of a storage-based supply than to refining the nature of such failure and asking why, for any specific type of use, a particular reliability is worth paying for; there has been far more concern with the possibility of trimming a fraction off future domestic demand – or even off estimates of such future demand – than with the pattern of re-use which converts our gross water uses into a much smaller net requirement. There are indeed broad expanses of the picture which we are only just beginning to fill in.

I have given some round figures of current water use (in its various senses) in England and Wales together with similar data about our natural

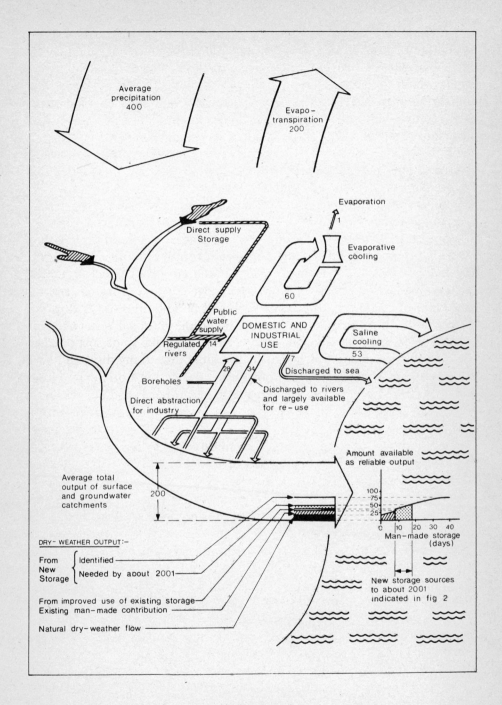

Fig. 1.1   England and Wales water balance
Simplified diagram showing principal quantities (millions m³/d)

7

water resources. This information is summarised in Figure 1.1. One may surmise that the flows which compose the domestic and industrial use pattern in that figure will roughly double by the end of the century. This will require an appropriate extension of the primary resource base, that is to say, a greater proportion of the average output of catchments will have to be converted, by storage, into reliable output. How much will depend upon growth of need; upon the pattern of re-use and circulation of fresh water; upon substitution of seawater; upon the need for residual flows at the mouths of rivers, and other factors.

Figure 1.2 indicates in outline a resource development pattern for England and Wales which would provide the requisite expansion of the resource base from ten surface storage units, together with managed groundwater zones. Some further local storage would be required in outlying areas. The adequacy of such provision to meet needs over the next thirty or forty years depends upon assumptions about the factors referred to above, and the validity of those assumptions will depend to a large degree on the policies of Regional Water Authorities. Such a pattern of development would interrelate with the management of the water cycle within each region; its usefulness and, indeed, its viability, will depend upon the relations which develop between regional authorities, and particularly upon their success in maintaining quality standards in the regulated river systems.

Discussion

Lord Zuckerman: The broad picture which we have been given is more than enough on which to build our discussion. Both Sir Norman and Mr Rydz have told us that there are many unknown variables in the equation for tomorrow.

I would like Sir Norman to tell us why he supposes, when one has this extremely ambitious programme for the provision of the water needs of this country to the year 2000, there will be other factors, such as those which determine the location of industry, which might negate the whole of this enormous system of investment.

Professor P.O. Wolf: I gather that a book on this seminar is to be prepared, and therefore I think it might be helpful to separate the facts, as far as one can be sure of them, from opinions and controversies. Would it be appropriate to start with establishing a few facts?

Mr Rydz was trying to bring out the question of extra storage yielding extra — let us tentatively call them — reliable supplies. If you have

2,000 million additional cubic metres of storage now and can produce from this 12 million cubic metres per day, then in the normal course of development a further storage volume of 2,000 million cubic metres in the same area by the principle of rapidly diminishing returns, will not give the twelve extra units. I am sure that Mr Rydz will want to point out that in the area where there is already a great deal of storage the provision of additional storage will not contribute substantially to reliable yield; but

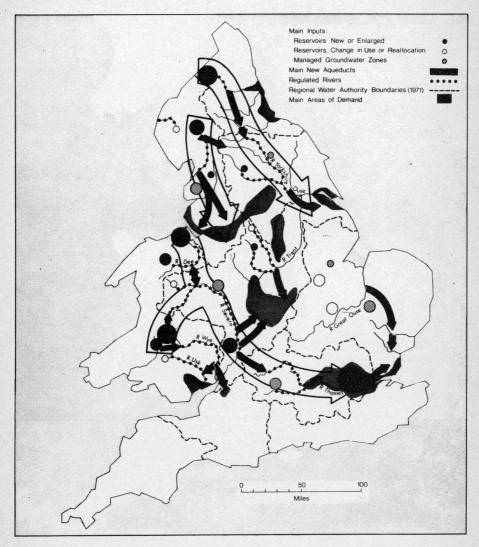

Fig. 1.2   England and Wales
Strategy for water storage and movement

there are large areas where there is so little storage that the provision of new storage will be as effective as has been claimed. I think this is a matter which is not very clear from the diagrams in the sense that the circles are not to scale in relation to the storage volumes.

Mr B. Rydz: It is of course true that increased storage in a catchment gives a diminishing return in yield. In the very round estimates I have given this is observed by several factors.

The new storage will be used almost entirely for regulation to serve abstraction points in the lower reaches of rivers. At these points abstraction conditions (i.e. residual flow requirements) will usually be quite different from those obtaining at upland direct supply points. Releases from storage will therefore be concentrated into shorter periods and the yield–storage relationship will be modified to give greater yields. In a number of cases the conversion to river regulation of existing direct supply or compensation reservoirs will greatly increase the maintained flow without any addition to storage. Manipulation of underground storage (not included in the estimate of new storage needed) is expected to contribute over a million cubic metres per day of new dry-weather flow. In all these cases one is in effect optimising the allocation of storage to the run-off pattern of the country, whereas in the past it has been allocated very unevenly and therefore inefficiently.

Professor P.O. Wolf: I accept that. Might I suggest that we accept all that Sir Norman said as historically accurate and therefore not controversial in a backward look, but that we should now think in terms of the forward look for the next thirty years, and extrapolate Sir Norman's introduction with population projections and in terms of water needs. The industrial use per capita is something that we should discuss and also the use of water per head of the population both as persons and as users of industrial products. I think that Sir Norman should be invited to expand this aspect. Can we arrive at a conclusion which will be helpful to the authorities and, incidentally, to scientists working in this field? I believe that the help that we are getting from our friends overseas will be interesting here, since their experiences may be in countries where either the pressures or the available resources are much greater.

The only other point I would like to bring forward at this stage is that there is a Hadrian's Wall across which no drop of water will pass and perhaps this might be touched on.

Sir Norman Rowntree: This is by and large a scientific gathering and no doubt it chooses, because it knows most about them, to talk about the scientific aspects, but scientifically and technically we have nearly all the answers. There are certain points which need further investigation and one

10

can save money by knowing more about them. But the big failure is in the administrative and financial system which will enable these scientific things to be developed. It would be helpful to highlight that.

Lord Zuckerman: I think that Sir Norman's remark is the valid one on which to focus, that technically we can manage, but there may be reasons why we will not manage. He has pointed to the weaknesses of administration but I suppose that these interact with others. In a debate on energy demands Lord Hinton said that one cannot estimate exactly what future energy demands will be.

Sir Norman Rowntree: Very early, when looking at this, we came up against this problem and decided that we need a system which is flexible. This made us look at rivers for the movement of water. One has not committed oneself to fixed points of abstraction or discharge, hence the attraction of the movement of water round the country in the river system so that one can meet changing situations. This liberty has to be available. The one gap — and here I am rather answering the question Lord Zuckerman posed at the beginning — is that we have no management over the pollution aspect at present. This is, of course, the essence of the current legislation.

Mr R. J. Bell: As Water Engineer for Norwich I think it might be appropriate for me to make a few comments at this stage from the practical point of view on our plans for the future and how these may be seen to fit into national planning.

To put the matter into perspective, from Norwich we control an area of seven hundred square miles in north east Norfolk with a population of 320,000. We became responsible for this enlarged area only two years ago so were able from the outset to draw up a plan for future supplies. Nationally this is not a problem area as far as water supplies are concerned and unless there is a very radical change in the pattern of development there will be no need to move large quantities of water to this part of East Anglia. We are sure that the answer lies in the proper development of local groundwater resources. We shall be able to supply water for possibly the next fifteen years by direct supply boreholes and then by river regulation schemes.

The present average demand per capita is about 0·180 cubic metres per day and by the year 2000 we consider this may have risen to 0·315 cubic metres per day. This projection was obtained from a study of our past consumptions and those of about fifty water authorities in south east England. It is difficult to be sure about projections of this sort and they must be revised from time to time but development programmes can be adjusted to suit changing circumstances. However, the point I want to

11

make is that we feel we can provide the supply required up to the next thirty years from local resources. I was interested to hear the earlier observations on other factors which can influence planning. This is a most important aspect because even during the last two months I have had to curtail my capital programme severely because of the Government's counter-inflation proposals and the freezing of water rates and charges. This may very regrettably have an effect on developments up to 1976.

Professor P. O. Wolf: I think that Mr Bell has followed my proposals that we should provide additional facts. Mr Bell has again brought the argument into the area which I think Sir Norman called 'not scientific'. Whether it is scientific, political, economic or social, it is a reality, and it is a reality which the new legislation will have to deal with, if not in 1974 then perhaps in 1984.

Mr D. J. Kinnersley: A number of speakers so far have shown what one might describe as impressive intellectual humility, but if we were talking about building the nation's power stations and were saying that we have got this programme for the year 2000, — is it wrong? — we shall not need it till 2010 — this would appear to be a somewhat casual attitude. Why are we taking this attitude? Is it because the capital investment in water is of very low intensity? Is it because we are dealing in very large units so that we have to speak of a ten-year margin of error? Is it because the forecasting techniques are poorly developed? It is unusual to conduct a conversation on the basis that a thirty-year forecast may be ten years wrong. In most industries this would be a surprising approach.

Lord Zuckerman: I find it normal. The difference in a discussion between academic and practical people is that when discussing a nuclear power plant, the academics will say that it can be built but that they know a better way of doing the job. When discussion begins, the practical men know that the project has already cost three times as much as it should have done, that it is already two years too late, that it is going to run into political trouble, and that the plant may not work. Were I to turn to the defence field there would also be some quite interesting comparisons.

I think this question is of the essence of planning. That is why I was interested to ask Sir Norman, in relation to one of his observations at the start, why he supposed that even if confident about the physical parameters for the future, you still cannot determine where industry is going to settle. It is because labour is the most important factor and you cannot determine where people are going to go in relation to a physical environment that has been created for them? I suppose you would call that an administrative problem.

Sir Norman Rowntree: I do not think it is capable of solution. We are

12

servants of the people and the people will want to determine their future. I do not think that in this country for a long time yet we are going to be able to tell industry where it must go or tell people where they should live. We have to create a system in which we can accommodate their wishes as far as we can.

Mr J. E. Beddoe: The strategy which Sir Norman and Mr Rydz are producing is designed as far as possible to minimise the risk by going for big resources, thereby giving greater flexibility in following whatever the pattern of development may be. You have to use a system which is as far as possible flexible in following the pattern of development.

Mr D. J. Kinnersley: That is a good answer. This margin of error which people have referred to is not a sort of residual but an objective, and I think that is a very good justification for it. I find that answer helpful.

Mr M. Nixon: I am not sure I agree with that. There are two factors which make forward planning very difficult. It currently takes about twelve years from beginning to completion of any major water resource project. In my view what is happening is that political influences are driving the planners into the selection of a few large sites which makes the other factor even more critical and therefore this reduces the flexibility. I am not sure whether we are right in going for these very large resources in the present political situation in practical terms although I am sure it is right in technical planning. But I am not very happy about the political side which does influence both the timing of these events and their size.

Mr B. Rydz: Mr Kinnersley suggests that a ten-year uncertainty in the timing of needs estimated for thirty years hence is excessive but I think few industries would care to be tied down even to that broad range of estimate.

Our purpose in planning is to choose the direction in which resource development should go and to test the choice against various imponderables. Will it prove sound if needs grow a lot faster or slower; if there should be a major shift in population; or if there were to be some other change in the premises of our argument? If it can accommodate all of these the direction or strategy can be chosen with some confidence.

How fast one will drive along the route in twenty years time is, for this generation, altogether a secondary issue. It demands our attention only if we doubt if the resource opportunities will be available or if we could meet costs of the magnitude involved. In water conservation these problems are unlikely to arise at least for several generations.

If we persuade ourselves that we can predict more accurately the needs and preferences of another generation this will, I fear, be no more than an exercise in self-deception.

13

The other point on which there has been some comment is the location of industry. These equations will hold good only if industry is located according to certain commonsense rules. I think this will happen. The most important user is the CEGB, who have indicated they are working on these lines: they will either go to sea or go to places where effluents are freely available and put in a lot more recirculation. There may be a few cases where factories which require substantial water services can be located rather more effectively downstream of a sewage works than upstream. It may be that here some new influence by the regional water authorities may have some part to play. But I do not want to suggest that the whole of this is likely to be overthrown because industry goes to the wrong places. I just stress that we have to start from sensible assumptions about what industry will do.

Mr J. E. Beddoe: Mr Nixon has a perfectly fair point. The more you commit yourselves to selection of a small number of large sources the more important is some long-term political undertaking. These are not problems of science, but they are problems of getting commitments which will only bite under the next government but two!

Dr A. L. Downing: May I take up a point that Sir Norman raised earlier about the political apparatus that we set up for managing this system and tie it into a remark that Mr Rydz made when he said that the national planning would be so much better than purely optimising on regions. Could Mr Rydz give us some indication of exactly how much better, because it is surely this that would determine the emphasis that we ought to place on the possibilities of changing the political format? I suggest that if one were able to optimise regionally and total up the water requirements, then halve the difference between that total and the national optimum to allow for the regional water authorities being co-operative to a substantial extent this might reflect the incentive for changing from an emphasis on regional planning to centralisation of planning. Has Mr Rydz any better measure of the difference between reasonable co-operativeness plus optimised regional planning and total national planning?

Mr Rydz referred to the various criteria and constraints by which the planning had to develop and mentioned the constraints on the use of reservoirs as one. He did not mention quality, but one feels that water quality must have been one of the inevitable constraints. I assume that must be so because he referred to the need to recycle within industry, and by implication he certainly ruled out direct recycling of reclaimed sewage effluent to the domestic consumer. Perhaps he could confirm whether that is the case or not, and whether quality considerations figure more generally in the optimisation.

14

As regards recycling in industry, could he indicate generally the way in which the industrial content of the scene would be managed? Could he give us an indication of how one is going to bring the individual requirements and attitudes of industry into a nationally optimised plan? For example, is the planning going to be determined and then industry told how much water it can have by edict, or is there going to be some kind of pricing policy?

Finally, I understand that the Americans are new seriously looking into the question of getting their water supply in California by towing icebergs from the North Pole. I think it was said that one 'jumbo-sized' iceberg would serve the city of San Diego for a whole year. Has anything of this kind been considered in our plan?

Mr B. Rydz: As to icebergs, I have no reason to believe that the idea of towing Antarctic ice sheets to California is altogether nonsense. But the ideas which have been canvassed and costed there are wholly out of scale with our modest needs; nor are we in the same extremity.

The opportunity to store water at strategic points and network it throughout England and Wales affects a comparatively small part of water cycle management as a whole. In its most economical forms it seems to offer cost savings equivalent to between £50 million and £100 million of current investment (i.e. discounted comparison) over equivalent provision by self-sufficient regions, disregarding various intangible advantages and disadvantages. But some additional costs will be accepted to reduce social impact and here a national pattern scores in reducing the number of reservoirs required and providing more alternative strategies. All depends, of course, on one's measure of gain or loss, but some actual programmes of development will be compared in our forthcoming report. I have always believed that a solution optimised nationally will have better promotion prospects, but experience does not wholly sustain that view as yet.

Water quality can be a major constraint on re-use for domestic purposes. This is already an important resource in south east England, although direct recycling of effluents to supply has not yet been contemplated. We have looked at the option of extending re-use by reclaiming the Trent to supply, but not, in specific cost terms, at the opposite course of abandoning, say, the Lee or the Great Ouse. We have assumed that the quality of all rivers must be maintained or improved but this cannot yet be linked directly into a cost optimisation of water conservation strategy.

Our assumptions about the pattern of industrial use have been pretty audacious, I think, since they require industrial location which will maximise the opportunities for re-use both of sewage effluents and industrial effluents. I believe that this will be achieved. But for this purpose we shall need to develop a positive approach to the design of industrial river systems by regional water authorities; close consultation with industrial users and planning authorities; and improved regulatory instruments including, I hope, quantity and quality charging schemes which will evoke the correct economic response from industry. Consultation must not be overlooked, because I do not think that a system of charges will suffice by itself. Basically we must surely try to signal to industry the information which will help it to take sound decisions for itself. In our general planning at the Water Resources Board we can do no more at this stage than try to assess what the outcome of all these processes will be in terms of the net impact on resources.

Mr J. E. Beddoe: Dr Downing has raised some fundamental questions. The planning we have done so far is only half of it. We have not had a system which could carry out properly planning of quality. There is also the very difficult question of the degree to which used water is acceptable as a source for drinking water in technical and medical terms and then in political terms. We are reaching the point where we are not certain whether some rivers will be of sufficient quality to be used as a source of potable water.

Mr D. Wilkes: With regard to the icebergs referred to by Dr Downing, these are glacial blocks from South Polar ice shelves. According to available evaporation rate calculations and the slow speed at which special tugs might pull them, enough unmelted ice could reach San Diego (assuming those calculations are right) for delivery at prices below those which Californians now have to pay for water in their arid areas. England does not yet have such high prices for water. On the contrary, your questions are: how do you avoid reaching the point where towing ice floes halfway around the planet is economical? and thus, what is the cheapest way to get more good water rather than what are all the physically possible ways to get it?

Dr J. Rees: It has been said that as the water industry is not a big spender it is of little significance if it undertakes capital investment prematurely. I find this approach misguided as the sums involved are not trivial. In south east England alone premature investment due to the over-forecasting of demands could add up over the next ten years to an overspending of £47 million in present value terms on capital account alone.

To date we have tended to blame our inability to forecast demands accurately on the variability of population trends, but this is by no means the full picture, as we have also failed to predict future levels of usage per capita. The lack of agreement on likely per capita demands can be strikingly illustrated by reference to the Welland, Nene and Ouse River Authorities, for which forecasts of daily municipal usage per capita in 1981 have varied from 0·27 to 0·37 cubic metres. Undoubtedly the main reason for the difficulties experienced in producing meaningful projections is the lack of research into the factors which determine the level of consumption. We do not yet have any clear idea of the quantitative relationship between water use and such critical variables as family composition, income, industrial growth or industry mix. Clearly this deficiency hampers the development of econometric forecasting models, and forces us to rely on at best crude extrapolations of past trends, or at worst on guestimates.

Finally, I must endorse the point made by Mr Nixon on the inflexibilities which result from 'thinking big' and planning investment in very large-scale units. Some consideration should be given to the possibility of developing a greater number of smaller schemes since available supply could be more closely adjusted to variation in demands. This would produce savings by reducing premature investments, and in present value terms such savings *could* outweigh the higher unit costs of the smaller scale schemes.

Lord Zuckerman: Is the proposition about a large number of small units rather than a smaller number of large units generally accepted? The point has been made twice.

Sir Norman Rowntree: When the Board was set up there were seven reservoirs in south east England proposed for investigation. There was such a controversy that we said we would reverse the procedure proposed under the 1963 Act, and instead of waiting for the River Authorities to bring their plans forward we would produce a plan for the region because of the demand for a comprehensive look at the system. We took a comprehensive look, and it produced a limited number of sources and an extremely flexible system for distributing the water from them. This was acceptable for a time. Now, both in the South East and the North East, we are being told to look the other way. We cannot go on in this country changing fundamentals of policy every ten years. The flexibility of the system is not in the number of sources but in the way you move the water from the sources.

Professor H. H. Lamb: Since margins of error have come up in planning, it needs to be put on record that up to 5 per cent error can be made in predicting the amount of rain nature will give over a decade; moreover this figure varies considerably between regions. The variability of rainfall is greater percentage-wise in the north west than in the South East.

Dr K. Smith: It has been suggested this morning that we know most of the scientific and technical answers, but there remain certain technical issues which are still not entirely clear. In particular, most of the discussion has centred on the estimation and forecasting of needs rather than the assessment of basic resources.

For resource estimation we have to look at the degree of success achieved by the hydrometric schemes instituted under the 1963 Act, because the emphasis in the 1963 Act was on quantities, and I feel that there are still several questions which our hydrometric network has yet to answer. Firstly, improvements in flow gauging were obviously necessary in 1963 but have become even more important because we are now clearly moving towards a management system where there is going to be a more direct relationship between quantity and quality. On the other hand, the fact remains that the lower reaches of most of our major river basins have never been gauged and we have, therefore, a lack of information about discharge characteristics of direct relevance in terms of barrage storage or estuarial pollution control. Secondly, Professor Lamb has already spoken about the variability of rainfall from year to year but there is also the question of the accuracy of rainfall measurement. We know that the standard rain gauge records less precipitation than actually reaches the ground nearby but I know of no work which attempts to interpret such point deficiencies on a catchment scale. In other words, what does this mean in terms of water resources assessment? Similarly, snow hydrology has been neglected in this country and we know very little about the implications of snowfall on a water resources basis.

Finally, I should like to make a point about the variability of river flows, because whilst we know a good deal about the average situation there has been very little work done on the study and simulation of extreme drought episodes. It seems to me that it would not be inappropriate that, to complement the recent floods' survey, some sort of droughts team should look at the implications of rainfall deficiencies at various times of the year and the effect of such dry-weather spells on different types of resources such as upland reservoirs, estuarial barrage storage and groundwater supplies. Certainly, as we come to rely increasingly on the planned conjunctive use of resources, we ought to have a better knowledge of how these different sources can be managed in an integrated fashion and how various hydrological parameters interact on the various types of resource.

Sir Frederick Warner: I want to go back to one of the earlier questions raised about the ten-year error that there can be in these predictions and what difference a system makes if you are doing present value studies. The essence of any study of present values or any attempt to decide between projects on the basis of things like discounted cash flow was first initiated in the chemical industry, where variations are much greater than the type

18

now being spoken about, namely, the 5 per cent errors in forcasting rainfall. Moreover, the industry as a whole is faced not only with great variations which arise from wild fluctuations in market demand but the great fluctuations imposed by new technologies. The kind of problem faced in planning is nothing to what industry has to face in doing a discounted cash flow calculation on a new proposal where the estimated life is ten years. The half-life of most technology is five years. When doing any discounted cash flow studies on these, you have got to take into account very big variations and allow for a much greater rate of writing off than in the type of industry connected with water supply and regulation. It is difficult for people from industrial disciplines to make forecasts over such long periods and with such a low provision for capital replacement. It is in this area that one sees the need for getting the kind of thing that Sir Norman has put up: you do in the end almost take a decision on what amounts to an engineer's vision.

Mr J. M. Boon: I am somewhat at a loss with so many scientific people present for I am a practical man who has had the job of supplying water for quite a large area for forty-three years. I wonder whether the planners could tell me how much their investigations and plans would have changed had more land been available for the conventional type of reservoir. For over a hundred years we have successfully put up a series of reservoirs which have met the needs of the immediate areas, and bigger ones could meet the needs of bigger areas. Many years ago I sat in front of Lord Greenwood, who was then Minister of Housing, when he was speaking about the cost of land for reservoirs and the opposition he experienced. There was a great deal of opposition from farming communities and much more from the people who love flora and fauna and sometimes get their priorities a bit wrong. I think that more land would have been available for the conventional type of reservoir if the farmers had been paid the right money for it. In my opinion the Ministry are taking the right line in regard to compensation to farmers, tenant farmers and people who are on the edges of motorways; the Ministry are taking a far more humane look at the damage done to these people. If the farmers' opposition to reservoirs were satisfied by the payment of what they, as well as the Ministry, might consider to be adequate compensation, how far would the plans change if the more coventional type of reservoir could be thought of for the period up to 2000?

Sir Norman Rowntree: The cheapest way to supply water to the end of the century would be to build very many reservoirs and ignore the question of land requirements. The problem is that if we reduced it to money terms, if we assume that people who have land would accept quite large sums of money, that would be the way to operate; but unfortunately it is not all a matter of money terms. There are very big human problems which money will not solve. There is no logical answer. The Board's approach has been to minimise the number of reservoir sites and minimise the number of problems for the politicians.

Mr D. J. Kinnersley: The pricing of land is very much a matter of convention and fashion. We have seen the price of agricultural land double in eighteen months. Normally, if you are exploiting resources like coal, it is conventional to speak of using the cheapest resource first, but land in this country is really a non-replaceable resource, and therefore its pricing is a matter of the utmost difficulty.

Mr J. M. Boon: It might be cheaper in the long run to buy vegetable produce from the Common Market and give the land over for water.

Mr G. W. Curtis: I am very intrigued by the criticisms of forecasting. For the last thirty years I have been building sewerage schemes and some water schemes in Norfolk; I sit in an office with the planners on the next floor, and on every scheme I get a planning projection before we start a design. I do not know one occasion when they have been right. This is not because they have not attempted to make a decent projection, but because you cannot forecast all human behaviour. There are so many other factors which enter into these things that I would find it quite impossible to say that you can forecast exactly what is going to be the pattern in this town or that village in future years. In that case, the more flexible you can make your overall policy, the better. The overall pattern seems to me to be an infinitely better approach than to rely on purely local parameters, because if the local organisation and the local provision does not work out correctly, then it is utterly devastating locally.

Lord Zuckerman: Dr Russell, you are going to speak later about the specific problem of planning demand and pricing problems. You are familiar with the USA position. Has anything that has emerged this morning indicated any difference in the way we in this, and you in your country, look at the whole problem?

Dr C. Russell: I do not think there is any difference in approach, except that, being geographically smaller, you can speak of a national system. We cannot do that in the USA. Some areas of comparable size, such as California, are building systems which are regionalised. In fact, exactly the same questions are discussed when people in the USA get together to discuss water; i.e. the question of forecasting, the question of pricing systems, the question of flexibility, and how you achieve it.

Mr B. Rydz: I think that if the resistance to land use for water storage were wholly removed, the pace of conversion to river regulation would relax somewhat, but nevertheless by the early years of the next century we would be in real difficulty in finding upland storage sites for direct supply. We would have some freedom of action for the next twenty to twenty-five years, but by then it would be vanishing. It is only the system of regulation of rivers and abstraction from their lower courses which gives us, at the present time, a choice from schemes which are adequate to meet about fourfold our estimated yields for the next thirty years.

Mr J. McLoughlin: We have heard a great deal about the difficulties of planners in trying to forecast, but I would comment that as far as land use development is concerned the planners not merely forecast but actually control. We need in the future a little more co-ordination between the control exercised and the forecasting done by planners.

Sir Norman Rowntree: The plans for land use only predict for ten or fifteen years by and large. By that time the water schemes on which we have to make decisions now have got to be completed.

Dr C. Russell: It seems to me that one of the contrasts between the USA and this country is that perhaps more research, particularly on the economic side, is done in the USA but there is not the machinery to make use of it which there appears to be here. We seem to know more, I think, but we have no institutions for making use of that knowledge.

Professor P. O. Wolf: Again trying to establish facts, I think I disagree with Dr Russell's last remark.

The main point I want to make is that we should give serious thought to what Professor Lamb and Sir Frederick Warner have said. Professor Lamb made the point that we could not forecast within, let us say, 5 or 10 per cent what is going to happen hydrologically. What we are concerned with is not rainfall but the water available, and if there is a variability in rainfall of 5 per cent, the variability in available water resource is much greater — 20 or 25 per cent. There is a multiplier here which, from the point of view of water resources, is very large.

Then there was Sir Frederick Warner's point that a forecast is bound to be a short-term one. Sir Norman Rowntree has dealt with this in terms of the accuracy of the short-term forecast and the inaccuracy of the long-term forecast, but in fact water is one of the most precisely known resources in terms of averages. Mr Rydz has dealt with averages. The temporal variability of the averages is not so well known, and we have no technique for saying in 1973 what is going to happen in nature in 1975. The forecasts of population are more accurate. The forecasts of demand per capita are far more flexible.

Lastly Sir Frederick has mentioned new technologies. This is an extremely important point which I think we should elaborate in another session.

Lord Zuckerman: The message that I have got from the discussion of this session is that what we·need are real plans and real action. We have got to accept the limitations of the data — the demand figures, the inadequacy of scientific data about flow patterns and of the other matters we discussed — we have got to take all these for granted and make the best sums we can. Somehow or other Mr Beddoe should be in a position in which — if necessary and appropriate — he can say to the Secretary of State for the Environment twenty years hence, 'We gave you the correct information, you did not act on it, and that is why this country is in such a mess now!'

2 Long-term Research Related to Development Programmes

V. K. COLLINGE

In some senses I have a rather daunting task, having had some insight into what we might see in the next thirty years, and all this in global terms, but nevertheless with some important and precise concepts; and I suppose in a sense it is a come down to talk about research and development, because this is sometimes used as the easy way out. If you cannot think of what to do next let us have a research and development programme! But, of course, our knowledge is not complete and adequate enough for the tasks that face us and in certain aspects I am sure that our needs for more precise knowledge are going to become very important. To take a completely different subject like bridge building, we know that, in spite of the enormous progress in materials and in design and construction methods, and all the research that we have had on these aspects and others, bridges still fall down. The reason, of course, is that all the time we are getting closer to the boundaries of our technological knowledge.

With regard to this country's water resources this has hitherto been far from the case. We have been well-endowed by Mother Nature, and we are dealing with systems which fortunately seem to contain large elements of safety in themselves. But I suggest that this situation is not going to exist for all that much longer. I believe that we are going to get progressively closer to the point where we will be pushing up against the limits, pushing our luck and judgement particularly in respect of water quality considerations, and for that reason I believe that we have substantial areas of research and development which will have to be covered if our plans for the future are going to be successful and operated with a minimum of risk.

I have set out a number of areas of lack of knowledge, and in dealing with these will concentrate on water quality, but I want to end by talking about some administrative problems, because at the end of the day if we have not got the right administrative organisation, no matter how clear and precise we may be about our research needs, we will find that they will not be accomplished in the way we would wish.

It is convenient to talk first about planning techniques. You have heard in the first session how strategic planning has been concerned with the quantitative element of water, with judgements based on experience on

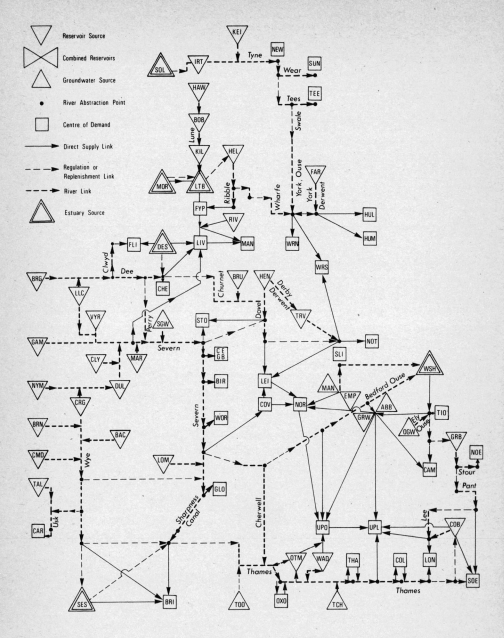

Fig. 2.1　Water resource developments in England and Wales — systems diagram

the suitability in terms of quality of river water for abstraction. Clearly, future programmes of effluent treatment must be prepared having regard to the proposed development of water resources and this brings new requirements for mathematical ways of studying and planning these actions. So far we have undertaken the development of mathematical models as planning aids based primarily on systems for looking at a wide range of possible combinations of resources, looking at these in quantitative terms only and identifying an optimum programme of development as well as a range of programmes of development with different constraints applied.

Figure 2.1 is a network diagram illustrating how this has been done in respect of the national study. There are squares which represent demands and a range of different triangular symbols which represent possible resources, and there are many links either by pipeline or by river. We now have mathematical ways of searching that network, and can identify an optimum programme of resource development, subject to any given constraints. Then we have more detailed methods for looking more precisely at a particular configuration and evaluating the costs in finer detail.

Figure 2.2 illustrates an entirely different type of model. This is a representation of a quality model developed for the River Trent. The river is divided into reaches and for each reach the quantity and quality of the flow in and flow out and of effluents coming in and abstractions are identified. We have a technique for searching through a number of reaches − in the case of the River Trent, thirty-three − and we can find alternative effluent treatment arrangements and their costs for achieving given or presumed quality conditions in the river. We may choose to put all our financial resources into upgrading one effluent, or may divide them between two or divide them in some way between all the effluents discharged, and we can search through these possibilities and find different solutions − we can also find an optimum solution. These are techniques which will need to be developed much further under the legislation that will operate from 1974. Furthermore, the ways in which industry uses particular rivers and the ways in which industry can harness the increasing effluents that will result from increasing water consumption, are areas of very imperfect understanding on which there must be much more intensive study of the sort illustrated here.

With that background, we can turn to the question of quality requirements. To my mind the highest priority for the future without doubt must be to determine much more precisely our quality requirements for water: first, for domestic consumption; secondly, for industrial consumption; thirdly, in situ in rivers; and fourthly, in situ in aquifers − and indeed Mr Beddoe has already touched on part of this in the first session. For

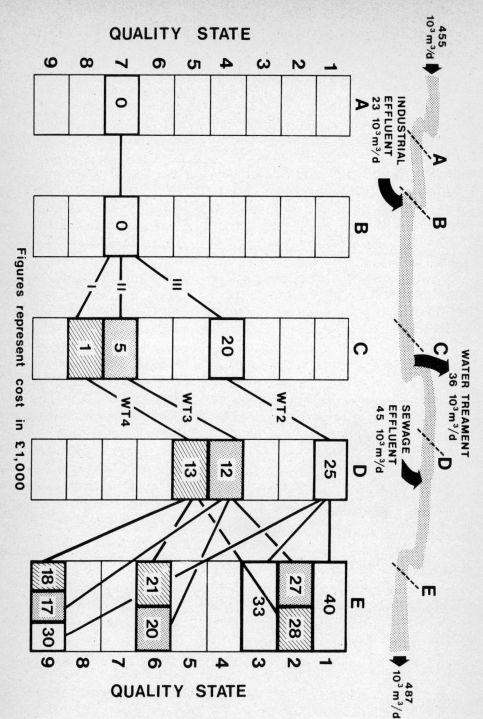

Fig. 2.2   Trent research programme — hypothetical example of the river model

26

reasons of time, I will concentrate on domestic consumption and in situ river needs.

On domestic consumption, the responsibility rests with the statutory water undertakings to supply wholesome water, and there is no definition of that. There are maximum allowable concentrations of various substances which are proposed by the World Health Organisation and the USA water quality criteria, but it is a fact that we have relatively little knowledge of the effects on the human body of substances which occur naturally and artifically in water. A number of these are currently under scrutiny, but if the sort of resource development plans we have heard about in the first session are to be realised, we must be much better informed on precisely what levels of substances are acceptable and what the risks of using water containing certain compounds are. To take, for example, hardness: there is an established statistical relationship between hardness and cardio-vascular disease. The relationship that has been established, however, is only statistical and not causal. There is as yet no medical evidence to back this up. Nitrates in excessive quantities can cause a blood disorder in infants, and in the River Lee the nitrates have risen to quite alarming levels. A little is known about the effects of cadmium, but we do not know how much a human body can tolerate or for how long before it does how much damage. Some of the blanket indicators that are used at present are but a very unsatisfactory substitute. Take as an example total organic carbon. It is very much a question of what are the sources of the organic carbon. Tap water in many places today contains 2 or 3 milligrams per litre total organic carbon, but in terms of using the River Trent with possible total organic carbon concentrations of 2 or 3 milligrams per litre after treatment to produce potable supplies this is looked upon as being highly desirable, and very understandably, because the source is very different. A cup of black coffee, has a total organic carbon of 2,500 milligrams per litre, and if it has sugar in it, it is a lot higher. It is a question of understanding and knowing what these organics are in much more detail.

This inevitably leads to the question of what quality is required in our rivers if they are to be used for public water supply. There are rivers used in this way at the present time, like the Derbyshire Derwent and the Bedford Ouse, which contain in dry-weather flow up to 75 per cent of effluents, or even more in extreme dry-weather conditions. On the other hand, we have looked at and considered the possibility of using the River Trent, which in quality terms, is far worse than either of those I have just mentioned. Now it has been rejected for the present, and I think, for sound reasons; but we must not forget that the Rhine, which is apprecia-

27

bly worse than the Trent, is used to supply Rotterdam.

If in the future we are able to define our required standards for drinking water and for industrial needs, then we have got to work out how to achieve these, and to bear in mind that there are important in situ river requirements like the maintenance of fisheries. Unquestionably amenity and recreation considerations, which we shall treat later, are going to play a very important role in our water resource developments over the next decades.

As to the consideration of effluent and water treatment, I will concentrate here on the effluent treatment side, and hope that Dr Allen will help us later on the water treatment side.

A recent article by Dr Downing in *Chemical Engineer* sets out clearly the situation that exists today in terms of the technology of effluent treatment in relation to our future needs. Basically we have knowledge of the methods that are available and could be developed on a full scale for achieving a wide range of different qualities of effluent. In other words, if you can say what quality of effluent you want, then a chain of processes can be prescribed to meet that requirement. I think that the most important needs, therefore, in our effluent treatment research and development work of the future lie much more with the engineering aspects of the processes than perhaps with the chemistry and biology of them. There are many aspects of the design and construction of these types of facilities which I believe are susceptible to considerable improvement — I speak now in economic terms — and I think that here we could see development programmes which could carry very high benefits, bearing in mind the enormous sums that will have to be spent on effluent treatment facilities in the coming decades.

A last point on the quality aspects relates to the distribution of water from treatment plants through the reticulation systems. We have heard strategies proposed which will inevitably lead to quite significant changes in the mix of resources with time. These are propositions which lead to changes in the quality of the water as received for treatment and distribution — perhaps quite significant changes — and I believe there is a need to study much further the consequences of those changes on the distribution systems and ultimately on the consumers.

There is then the very important question of how we are going to utilise existing and new reservoirs and groundwater resources in order to derive the maximum benefit from them. The traditional methods of water conservation by direct supply from surface reservoirs and underground storage have given way to three new concepts. First, river regulation by upstream reservoirs; second, river regulation by groundwater abstraction and discharge to rivers; and third, the combined or conjunctive use of resources. Each of these subjects is in its infancy and must be taken to much more refined limits in order to first, make the maximum use of those resources, and, second, be sure that we are utilising them within the true limits of availability of the resource. To get back to the anaology with bridges; over-refinement and over-sophistication could take us to the point of delusion and deception and then the day of reckoning would come.

River regulation by upstream storage is, of course, already used, and the River Dee is a working example. One of the major limitations of developing a system of this sort, particularly if the storage can be used for flood control, is that of weather forecasting. It is not too difficult to forecast the flows in a river given that you know how much rain is falling or has fallen on the catchment. This is the hydrological, and the easy, half of the problem. What is difficult is knowing how much is going to fall – and we all know this difficulty. However, this subject is being explored and gradually advances are being made. We must bear in mind that the sort of forecast time we are talking about can be quite considerable. Probably an extreme example is the River Severn where in dry weather it can take three days for releases from the reservoir to reach the downstream lengths of the river, and so ideally one wishes to forecast over a three-day period what the flows in that river system will be. This cannot be done at present. There have been, however, quite exciting developments on the meteorological front with the advent of mathematical models of the atmosphere and these are now being used by the Meteorological Office in its routine forecasting work. On another scale there is also the development of weather radar. A weather radar system has been installed on the River Dee by the Meteorological Office, Plessey and the Water Resources Board, and is now being used quite effectively to measure rainfall. The system has not yet advanced to the stage of assisting in the forecasting process, but this will follow, and perhaps some combination of the atmospheric model for the longer term, the radar for the medium term and a local system for the very short term will eventually enable us to give quite reasonable predictions of future river flows.

I have talked a little about groundwater and would like to illustrate how developments are already enabling us to make greater use of our groundwater and to show the ways by which groundwater can be harnessed to a much greater extent. While Mr Rydz was talking about storage requirements for the future, he quoted a figure of 2,000 million cubic metres. Now, very roughly, the storage in our aquifers – the total volume – is of the order of 10,000 million cubic metres. Of course vast amounts of this are not available so this cannot be taken in any sense as a direct

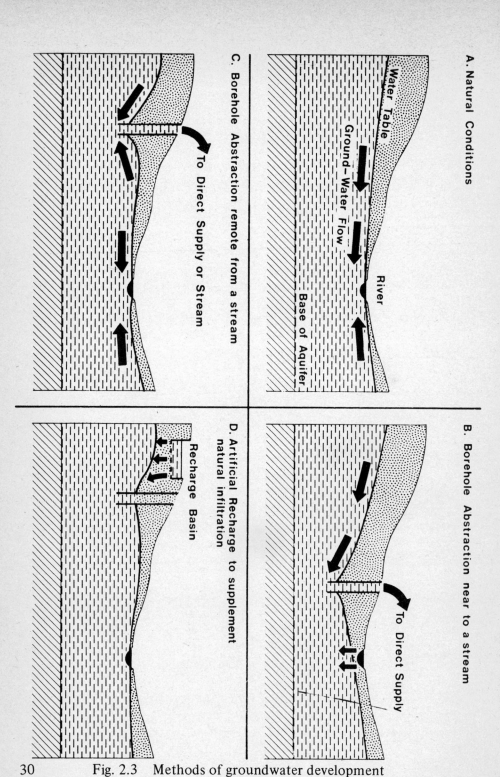

A. Natural Conditions

Water Table

Ground-Water Flow

River

Base of Aquifer

B. Borehole Abstraction near to a stream

To Direct Supply

C. Borehole Abstraction remote from a stream

To Direct Supply or Stream

D. Artificial Recharge to supplement natural infiltration

Recharge Basin

30　　　　Fig. 2.3　Methods of groundwater development

comparison, but the figures do show the enormous volume of storage that exists underground. The following section illustrates now this can be more effectively utilised.

Figure 2.3 shows diagramatically methods which are currently being explored for the more effective use of groundwater. Traditionally a borehole is put down, and water abstracted at a more or less constant rate and this is taken to direct supply. By removing that borehole to a point remote from the river it is possible to abstract water and put it into the river, and to carry this out only for relatively short periods when river flows are naturally diminished. It is a redistribution of the river flows with time, but the effect is that you can draw more heavily on that river downstream for abstraction purposes, and when the natural flows are not adequate you can draw on the storage of the aquifer temporarily, pump it heavily, put the water in the river to sustain the river flow, and then in the winter cease pumping, naturally recharge and take the levels back up. Two pilot schemes have already been carried out and a prototype scheme is now authorised which will yield up to 0·5 of the 10 or 12 million m³/day that Mr Rydz seeks. A similar scheme will be promoted in the Great Ouse area which will yield a somewhat lower but not dissimilar figure.

Two important points follow from this. First, there are other aquifers which can be used in this way. Taken together, these might yield about 1·2 million cubic metres per day, so there is great scope here. Secondly, from the research and development point of view operational experience with one such scheme is badly needed. At present, investigations are being carried out in many aquifers, but there is no operational experience and there are bound to be unexpected pitfalls. Leading from this, a lot of energy will need to be devoted to developing the operational rules for operating a system of this sort, a system which will require many boreholes over a wide area, all to be remotely controlled. Again there is the question of forecasting river flows, so there may be some long-term forecasting problems as well as relatively short-term ones.

As to the question of the combined use of resources, Figure 2.4 illustrates a point here. It is a diagrammatical representation of the Welland and Nene river system. This depicts the system concept, and it is now vital that these systems are looked at in this way and not as they have hitherto been as isolated pockets of development. To illustrate the effect of looking at the system approach, let me quote three figures from the study we have done based on that diagram. The yield from Empingham, without considering the effluent returns, is 230,000 m³ per day. If effluent returns are included this could become 475,000 m³ per day. There are very impor-

31

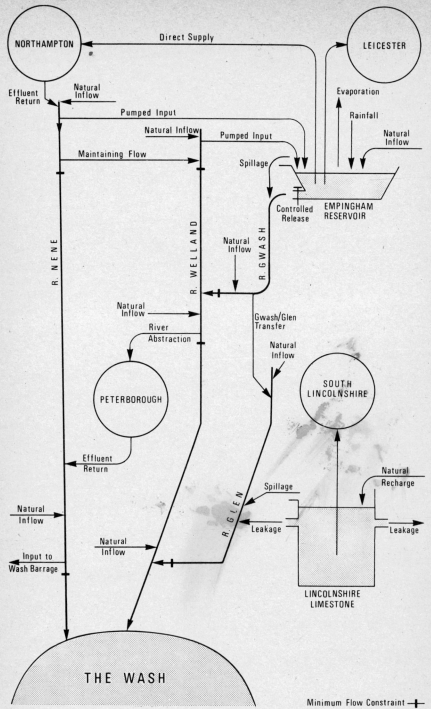

Fig. 2.4   Welland and Nene resources system — simulation diagram

tant qualifications which go into that, of course, bearing in mind what I have said about water quality. If that system is used in conjunction with the Lincolnshire limestone, there will be something near 600,000 m³ per day of total available water. Those figures underline the importance of using the system concept.

Turning to new types of resources, the bottom right hand diagram of Figure 2.3 illustrates the ultimate stage of the development of ground water by recharge. The natural use of ground water carries the limitation of what nature provides. This sort of system cannot in the long term abstract more than nature puts in, but storage can be used to increase artifically the availability of water. Water can be put in by recharge, either from basins or through wells, and the water used for this purpose usually comes from a river in times of surplus. We are back to the storage question. Can water be taken in times of surplus, put into the aquifers, and drawn upon in times of deficit? In fact, recharge is also used as a purification process if the basin system is used.

In this country there are considerable possibilities here. These techniques are widely used in certain overseas countries, like Germany and Sweden, but mainly in superficial deposits, whereas in this country the interest lies in deeper-lying aquifers. So far efforts have been concentrated on three areas – the London basin, where the story of the decline of water levels is well known, Nottinghamshire, and an area in Sussex. The additional yield that might be possible from those three situations could be about 0·8 million cubic metres a day. But there are other areas in the country where this technique might find application, as, for example, the Vale of York. It could be that the natural sequence would be one of river regulation first, followed by a recharge, as an ultimate stage of development.

The studies involved in recharge are very considerable and must follow this order: first, study of the hydrogeology of the situation; secondly, mathematical modelling in order to understand the way in which the aquifer behaves; thirdly, engineering and economic studies; fourthly, field experience through putting down boreholes or building recharge basins in order to test the theories; and finally, a prototype scheme.

In an experimental basin at Edwinstowe water has been taken from a small tributary, pumped through pipes for about a mile, given simple aeration and put into the recharge basin. We have been carrying out recharge experiments there for two years now jointly with the Trent River Authority.

This is the easy part of the task; it is relatively small-scale, inexpensive work. We must get prototype schemes. Now to the steep part of the curve.

Will the Lee Conservancy carry out a prototype scheme in the Lee Valley? Will there be a prototype scheme in the Trent area? That is what we must move to.

Under the heading of new resources I now come to desalination. There are two things about desalination. A basic research and development programme must be maintained for two reasons. First we must be in the position of having the technology when we need it, although that will not be for quite a long time; but secondly, and more important, we have got to satisfy amenity interests that the subject is being properly looked at. It would be a good investment to spend £ 100,000 a year because we might save ourselves a lot of money in other respects.

In the interests of time I must leave aside the question of ecological effects of water resource systems. Work on this subject will have to be intensified and should take place through a shift from basic research on freshwater biology to applied studies. More information is badly needed on the biological effects on rivers of changes in the flow regime, particularly by river regulation and interbasin transfers.

In the remaining time I shall deal very quickly with two questions of administrative problems. First, the Government has proposed a new Water Industry Research Centre which will be paid for and run by its members, mainly the Regional Water Authorities. I would support that very strongly but see formidable problems in creating this in terms of staffing, finance, programme of work, and so on. These are urgent problems, problems of today and not of tomorrow, which must be tackled energetically.

Table 2.1

NERC research grants to universities current at 31 March 1971
and research studentships in 1971

Subjects	Grants	Studentships
	£ 000's	
Meteorology	192	13
Hydrology	166	15
Oceanography and fisheries	815	55
Nature conservancy	315	35
Land use	71	3
Forestry and woodland	252	10
Geology and geophysics	2,880	130

Secondly, there is the question of how to change the direction of research and development effort. It seems that one of the big problems we face administratively is the enormous difficulty of changing something that is rolling in one direction to something that rolls in another direction. As an illustration, I reproduce in Table 2.1 some figures relating to the research grants given by the Natural Environment Research Council to universities. It shows that the universities are given a paltry £166,000 on hydrology, but nearly £3 million goes on geology and geophysics. In terms of studentships, these add up to 131 on things like forestry, hydrology, woodland and land use, and 130 for geology. These figures surely do not reflect our needs for the future.

Discussion

Lord Zuckerman: We have been given a very wide choice of topics for this discussion. Mr Collinge began with the indication that while there are criteria by which one attempts to satisfy the requirements for wholesome water; in point of fact most of them are speculative. I would like to reinforce that view. I myself think many of our criteria have been invented arbitrarily over the past decade. There is regrettably little real science in this field, and much public emotion.

Dr R. G. Allen: One must agree wholeheartedly with nearly everything that Mr Collinge has said. He referred to the inadequacy of our medical understanding of the implications of contaminants in the water that we drink. He implied, as Lord Zuckerman implied, that in order to resolve those problems the research back-up must be long-term. It must take ten years or more to establish the likely effect of a particular organic in drinking water upon the health of consumers. How can one agree with Mr Rydz, who is telling us to re-use it all and, by implication, admitting that the organics will go up, when we need at least ten years breathing space to find out whether he is doing the right thing? This is indeed a difficult problem.

Mr Rydz spoke of the most water for the least cost, but the problem is to recognise in the planning the desire to provide also for the best. The expectations of consumers everywhere are rising; we can afford a higher standard, and we demand it. Would the man in the street really want all this second-hand and third-hand water we are being offered for the future, if he knew that he could have first-hand water? It would cost him more, but he could pay it. I believe it is necessary to emphasise this point, since it relates to the very objectives of our planning.

We found on the Trent study, to which Mr Collinge referred, that advanced water treatment would cost only about 10 per cent more than conventional water treatment. The margins there are not very great. On the other hand, however, first-hand water would cost approximately 10 per cent more than the second-hand water obtained from advanced water treatments. If this is so, one's interest must be strongly attracted to the surplus water resources of Scotland. There is a great deal of excellent water in Scotland. Of course, there are also some hills in the way, but it is very likely that the man in the street would be quite prepared to pay to have it pumped over them. I repeat, this is a principle to which we must give serious attention.

Mr Collinge asked me to comment on water treatment processes. The position is that present processes do not, and cannot, remove all those unknown organics which the medical people are worried about. If it becomes necessary, two extra stages will be added to conventional plant; treatment with activated carbon, and probably ion exchange as well. These are quite major processes and must add significantly to treatment costs.

I agree with all Mr Collinge's points about future lines for research. I do not entirely agree with his priorities relating to recharge; I would put considerations of water quality earlier on the list, probably first. But there is another area which we must not forget when talking about the treatment of water or of sewage, that is, how to dispose of the material removed from the treated water? Heavy metals are injurious to health and we know how to get them out, but there is need for considerable research into the disposal of them and other effluents.

Lord Zuckerman: You said that you would pay 10 per cent more to get a better article, but you started off by saying that you did not know what you would be buying. Why then do you want to pay more?

Dr R. G. Allen: We have got to know. Historically we have known, because it has been the practice of the water industry to go into the hills or underground and get the best that is available. Having used that for a decade or so, we can use the medical statistics for the population and find confidence in that, because an absence of medical troubles attributable to water is the goal. There has been no major outbreak of waterborne disease in this country in recent decades except for the Croydon epidemic. Thus we know that the water engineer up to the present time has been doing the right thing, although he did not know the scientific detail of why he was doing it. He still does not know, but now we have Mr Rydz telling us to go down to the estuaries, dam those off and drink all the water that everybody has polluted right the way down. This we do not know about.

Some of you may think there is more science in this business than there really is. The World Health Organisation sets down standards which define eleven parameters; in the waterworks we currently measure eighteen. There are about a hundred elements in the earth. An enormous number of compounds having different characteristics are now discharged by industry. Thus, there are many things that we do not measure. This has been all right historically, there has not been the need to monitor these things, but if we are going to accelerate greatly the rate of re-use we have got to do a lot more. Russia has water quality standards for surface reservoirs, other standards for distributed water, and also standards to give a water which would support health and not merely prevent disease. In their ordinary water quality standards they list 294 materials. This is because in Russia they are backing up the water quality aspect with a very considerable medical programme, and many of those 294 materials have been evaluated against toxicological and epidemiological considerations. They have started on this ten-year stint, and I think we must really get started in this area ourselves.

Sir Norman Rowntree: There are only two medically qualified people in this country directly concerned in water supply. The medical profession by and large gives little attention to water as a subject for preventive medicine.

Dr R. G. Allen: There is the reverse situation too. I am on the Environmental Panel of the World Health Organisation, and in the World Health Assembly, which is full of doctors. There is only one nation that ever sends engineers to that assembly, and that is America. This is very bad, because what the engineer does has so large an effect upon the medical quality of the water supplied. This matter also needs looking into.

Lord Zuckerman: When you speak of only two doctors, Sir Norman, do you mean research medical people?

Sir Norman Rowntree: The Metropolitan Water Board has for a long time had a medical man at the head of its water quality organisation, and I believe the Department of Health and Science has a doctor who devotes his time to this matter. I know of no other full-time doctors on water supply matters.

Dr R. G. Allen: We must not forget the Public Health Laboratory Service.

Lord Zuckerman: Are not epidemiological studies being carried out in different parts of the country into the incidence of certain diseases in relation to heavy metals in water supplies?

Sir Frederick Warner: I should have thought that the Metropolitan Water Board chemist responsible for the supply to millions of people, had sampled some of the worst water that there is. They are coping with water which has up to 500 milligrams per litre of dissolved solids which is re-used about four times. They have already got to grips with water which one would say is of very low quality and which has been accepted for a long time by the largest section of population of this country.

Lord Zuckerman: With a greater average longevity.

Dr A. L. Downing: It is not difficult to see the dilemma, and it is one that I suspect will not be resolved in this country for many years. Our existing practice is in a sense an experiment which has been going on, as Sir Frederick Warner indicated, for the last fifty years. I think the impor-tant thing we have got to watch is that we do not forget that the situation is not stable. What is going into the sewers now is not the same as was going in ten years ago. I think it would be unrealistic to suppose that we can ever measure everything that is there and have it tested epidemiologic-ally and physiologically.

I think that one must choose some pragmatic middle course and at least get some techniques for fingerprinting what is in a purely domestic sewage effluent so that one can distinguish that from new industrial components. If one can satisfy oneself that broadly speaking normal domestic sewage is all right for drinking up to whatever percentage it might be, that gives some sort of base line; one can then monitor the situation so as to reveal changes and then question their significance.

If I may refer to Mr Collinge's paper, something he said — although I think I know what he meant — was a little inconsistent in relation to this particular point. He was pointing to the need for the dose-response curves which one would ideally like to have. On the other hand, he was saying that we do not really need to know much more about chemistry of effluent treatment plants. But, of course, it is the chemistry of effluent treatment plants which determines exactly what these substances are go-ing to be. As you find out more about them, you have got to go back to the effluent treatment system and look at the chemistry and how it deter-mines what comes out in order finally to optimise the system.

Lord Zuckerman: Dr Allen's question about what is done with the material removed from the water has not yet been answered.

Dr A. L. Downing: Again, I think it is easy to overstate the problem of sludge disposal. One is up against the uncertainty of the ecological impact of things like heavy metals, and so on, but there is a great deal of past experience which does not suggest that the situation and our present practices are all that frightening. A study of the possibilities of increasing the rate of dumping of sludge in Liverpool Bay by a factor of six has just been completed, and although I think that everyone engaged in that study would agree that it left a number of loose ends, nevertheless the overwhelming conclusion was that it was reasonable to continue this dumping up and to increase the rate by up to sixfold, provided one coupled this with a monitoring system to check that unforeseen changes were not taking place. Generally speaking, similar margins of safety may well be true of other sludge disposal operations. Much is known about the effect of heavy metals on agriculture and one arranges disposal so that one does not exceed the permissible limits. I do not minimise the fact that there are problems, but at the same time I think it is easy to over-estimate them.

Dr R. G. Allen: I think the point Dr Downing is making is well taken. We do have the techniques for disposing of waste materials effectively. I was merely making the point that if medical science gets us down to recognising that an intake of half a part per million of cadmium is injurious to health, then we have to take it out of the water. We have then to put it somewhere where it does not matter. Dumping in the sea seems to be an answer, but this is not always practicable or desirable.

Mr D. Ruxton: I have been involved for some time with schemes for the storage of water in estuaries, and I am always a little worried about thresholds. One knows from experience that people have different thresholds. On the River Dee, some of those people who have complained in the past about the water supply having a taste are taken onto a panel who go out in boats in turns and taste the raw river water before it goes through the Chester Waterworks Company's treatment plant. This is a time-honoured way of seeing whether that particular water is satisfactory. If one were to choose at random another group of citizens to sit in the boat, there might be no response to taste at all. With some people the thresholds are much lower than with others.

On the question of Rotterdam and the use of the Rhine, I was told by Dutch engineers that they are changing from that source to the Meuse. This is one of the big features of their Beisbosch scheme. They consider that moving to a catchment which is only 40 per cent of the area of the other one, they have a better chance of controlling pollutants. They also say that it is less industrialised. The Dutch engineer I spoke to said he considered that the dilution of wastes was not enough and that it was better to use a catchment where effluents did not occur, if possible.

When Mr Collinge spoke about research and development, he suggested that it was often introduced as a means of putting off unpleasant decisions and delaying the making of choices. My firm's view of research is that it is a means of reducing the number of pitfalls in developing particular schemes, and our research should be designed with this end in view.

With regard to quality, we have been on the fringe of a study which is going ahead in the Great Ouse catchment. Models have been proposed to represent quality changes, and we have been considering what might be done with specific elements of catchment areas to try to discover and measure the compounds which come from agricultural areas into the rivers. In the Wash catchment the agricultural element is the primary one. Small catchment studies and plot studies are proposed to show first, what comes off the land naturally and secondly, how this might change over time with changing agriculture and management of the land. At present, the water is not badly polluted but there are serious problems, because of the interaction of chemical, physical and biological elements all the time in every stretch of the river. The problem will thus be difficult to resolve. Not enough is known at present about the substances going in. We accept that quality measurement is satisfactory at a particular stage of river use, but we would say that as the use becomes intensive it is better to measure what goes in so that a mass balance can be established, measurements being made of the substances deriving from factories, domestic or urban effluent plant.

Sir Frederick Warner: If we are going to talk about what goes into systems, I think it would be as well to take advantage of the work done in the Thames estuary. In general, although we have quite a high concentration of all sorts of things, we might say that the aspect really responsible for most of the troubles is still the lack of proper treatment of domestic sewage. This is still our major problem. People talk about industry and the effects of industrial waste. I would have thought the major problem was still domestic waste, this being rapidly approached by the sort of effluents that we get from factory farming and large-scale production in agriculture. The kind of research programmes that Mr Collinge was talking about would seem to give us some of the most difficult of long-term problems without trying to identify what the priorities are. What are the priorities? I wonder whether we could have some comments from those qualified to speak on what research problems they can identify which can be tackled in a reasonable time.

Mr H. Richards: In our programme there is a mention of something 'leading to a fairly well defined research programme'. It is very difficult to say anything in any sort of detail, but I will try to summarise the approach of some of us to this whole problem of assessing resources, developing them with acceptable effects on the environment, and providing information for future managemant.

It seems to me there are three broad categories. First, we need to understand the relevant parts of the hydrological cycle which we need to know something about now. One of them already touched on is how much water actually is available at the surface of the ground. This is very relevant to the problem of assessing groundwater resources. In the eastern part of the country an error of one inch in measuring the infiltration actually available to the ground can make a difference of between 20 and 40 per cent in the estimate of groundwater resources. Another thing which is relevant is the problem of infiltration and movement to the unsaturated zone. What happens between the ground surface and water getting into the main body of ground water? What factors bring about changes in the chemistry of groundwater? We have surely, as part of the study of the hydrological cycle, to consider the occurrence and movement of surface and groundwater. When looking at groundwater one is sampling at points in the same way as one samples rainfall at points.

The second group of problems seem to be methods of collection and processing of the relevant data. There is an enormous amount of research needed in this field.

Thirdly, there is the protection and management of water resources. There is no shortage of ideas among the scientific and technical people concerned with these, but many of them are working in quite separate groups, and we find that some of them seem not in any way to be working towards a practical end. The information seems to be scattered among a wide range of literature, and this raises the whole question of information services which are suitable for passing on what is being done by other people.

My own field of interest is groundwater, and I do not want to enter into debate with my colleague about the role of geology, but I agree with his general comment that there could well be a greater effort in the geological field in going into some of the problems relevant to groundwater and surface water relationships. This is of direct relevance to all of us. The movement of water from the surface to the groundwater is very complex and involves a knowledge of physics, microbiology, chemistry, hydrology, and so on, but the science which is concerned here is relevant to a wide range of problems. It is not only the recharge from rainfall which replenishes the aquifers; the problem is also what we do with some of the effluents which flow into polluted rivers and, in certain circumstances, are taken into the aquifers. Therefore, the movement of toxic and other pollutants is very relevant.

We know little about the factors controlling the chemistry of groundwater. We have been given some idea of the quantities involved, but we are dealing with a three-dimensional system which varies very rapidly in many cases, and because of this problem of sampling only at points our knowledge of the variation is very limited, and if we are going to make the most use of the storage that is available underground — and it has the advantage of being able to be developed in stages to meet increasing demand — we have got to know a lot more about the variation in chemistry so that the water engineer who has to put water into supply can predict exactly what kind of water he is going to obtain, within limits, if the carries out particular works. This raises the whole problem of hydrological prediction in general.

Mr D. J. Kinnersley: May I return to one thing that Sir Frederick Warner said to Dr Allen's remarks? Dr Allen made an attractive plea for first-hand water from Scotland. What slightly troubled me about this argument is that if we go on getting more and more first-hand water, when we have used it it will still be second-hand water, so that we shall be vastly increasing our stock or flow of second-hand water. It seems to me that we have to have a policy for that which is basically a sewage treatment policy related to a policy of taking a lot of first-hand water, if we were to pursue that. I do not feel that procuring water from Scotland would in any way reduce the importance — in fact it would in some ways increase the importance — of the treatment problems that are being discussed.

Professor P. O. Wolf: I am entirely in favour of quality control, and I plead for the diversion of clean water so that we arrive at the best overall system, namely water in the right quantity and quality where and when needed.

Dr A. L. Downing: This is just one aspect of the problem of increasing population and increasing water usage. It does not matter where one brings the water from, if one is going to use more of it one will have more waste water. If one is going to maintain the state of flow of any river in which the discharge of waste water is to be increased, it is axiomatic that one must tighten the effluent standards to maintain the condition as it was. So the question really is, are there methods available to do that? I think there is no doubt that there are, at least judged in terms of the traditional parameters by which effluent quality is measured. For example, if it were simply a question of maintaining the BOD of the water, then there would not be any great difficulty about that. For another 5p per thousand gallons one could reduce the BOD of effluents to about a quarter or a fifth of that now accepted as the norm. Broadly speaking, this is true of most of the other parameters by which effluents are currently judged, it is largely a matter of spending more. Certainly one has to have a guiding policy, and models like the Trent study give the framework to decide that policy.

Lord Zuckerman: Have you a clear idea, Mr Collinge, of what biological work would be needed to establish criteria in a more scientific way than that of today?

Mr V. K. Collinge: With regard to the biological condition of our rivers and the in situ requirements – or are you referring to water quality for potable supplies?

Lord Zuckerman: I am not speaking about ecological problems. I am talking about danger to the ultimate consumer of unwholesome domestic water. How would you set about persuading the Medical Research Council that this is a really important problem? I imagine that they give few research studentships to people working on water quality in comparison with those working on cancer. Is there a research programme on the biological side?

Sir Frederick Warner: You dismiss the ecological condition?

Lord Zuckerman: Only in this context.

Sir Norman Rowntree: At the present time, because of the lack of precise scientific knowledge, the water engineer relies on the ecological condition of the river. The fish are the only reliable indicator of the absence of a dangerous pollutant at the present time. The water engineer is very interested in the maintenance of good ecological conditions.

Mr J. E. Beddoe: One of the things we need as administrators is more help in getting the answer to the question of 'what is a wholesome water?' One of the problems is asking the right questions. Until we do that we cannot make a sensible approach to research.

Sir Norman Rowntree: In each of the Board's regional reports we have said that these plans depend on keeping the rivers clean. This was not a Water Resources Board function, and it was impossible to indentify who, other than the Secretary of State, is supposed to deal with it.

Mr B. Rydz: The problems of water re-use have been remitted to the Medical Research Panel set up to look into this. It was difficult to find the terms in which to remit the problem, and it has been remitted in most general terms by the Water Quality Steering Committee of the department. We could not identify the causes of our anxiety, and the problem was simply put in general terms: the re-use of water is increasing – will you look at it and tell us what you think are the matters of concern? It is an open-ended question.

Lord Zuckerman: You will get an open-ended answer. I suspect.

Mr V. K. Collinge: In closing the discussion I will concentrate on answering two or three specific points. The discussion has been a stimulating and self-generating one. Dr Allen raised a point at the outset in respect of chemistry problems in relation to artificial recharge, and it is true that I glossed over this, but only in the interests of time, because I did identify four water quality requirements of which underground water as one of the four. I had by no means forgotten it.

Mr Ruxton rather had the impression that I regarded research and development as a means of putting off decisions. As a director of a research and development programme, that is the last thing I would regard it as being. Of course we use it as a means of avoiding pitfalls. It is just that some people prefer to use it in the other misdirected way.

It has been suggested that one of the solutions to my rather provocative set of figures was to use some of the geologists on underground water problems. This is not the point I was getting at. I want to see some of the geologists turned into medical men to answer Lord Zuckerman's point. It is the direction of effort that we have got to shift, and how we do that is indeed a formidable problem — which leads me to my last point.

I was asked by Sir Frederick Warner what are my priorities. I have set out a lot of difficult problems. We have done most of the easy things. We have now got some challenging and extremely difficult problems to solve, and my priorities are the ones I set out in my talk. I have left aside all sorts of peripheral issues like demand forecasting, measuring, river flow, instrumentation, data transmission, and so on. I gave my priorities in my talk. These are the things which I believe have got to be done, and I feel that the sense of the discussion was essentially to endorse that. For that I am grateful.

3 Protection and Treatment of Supplies

Sir FREDERICK WARNER

Pollution Legislation

The control of waste dispersal, including sewage, is effected principally through a variety of statutory enactments, although Common Law has had some surprising successes in asserting the rights of individuals against polluters (e.g. *Pride of Derby Angling Association Ltd* v. *British Celanese Ltd and others*).

The Public Health Act, 1936, gave powers to local authorities to control nuisances and specifically required them to provide public sewers and to deal effectively with the collected effluents. The Drainage of Trade Premises Act, 1937, required local authorities to accept trade effluents, and conferred powers to improve conditions and make charges in respect of discharges, except for those made before the Act and not substantially altered. The Public Health Act, 1961, brought even these discharges under control.

River Boards were set up under the Rivers (Prevention of Pollution) Acts, 1951 and 1961, and these, together with the Clean Rivers (Estuaries and Tidal Waters) Act, 1960, gave them power to control effluents discharged to non-tidal rivers pre- and post-1961, fresh discharges to tidal waters after 1951, and post-1960 discharges to tidal waters and parts of the sea at estuary mouths defined as 'controlled waters'. Powers of the River Boards, together with new powers relating to discharges to underground strata, were transferred under the Water Resources Act, 1963 (amended in 1968 and 1971 to twenty-nine new River Authorities. Certain other provisions relating to water pollution are contained in the Salmon and Freshwater Fisheries Acts, 1923–65; the Sea Fisheries Regulation Act, 1966; the Oil in Navigable Waters Acts, 1955–71; and the Deposit of Poisonous Waste Act, 1972.

Success of Control

Under the Water Resources Act, 1963, River Authorities are required to license polluters and water abstractors according to the provisions of the Rivers (Prevention of Pollution) Acts, 1951 and 1961, and the Clean Rivers (Estuaries and Tidal Waters) Act, 1960. They are also required to undertake a hydrometric scheme to estimate and plan water resources, to undertake flow measurement and to publish an annual report. They must also determine and estimate the capacity of certain underground water supplies.

What then have been the results of this legislation? A comparison of a survey of river pollution in England and Wales in 1970, and one in 1958, shows that the length of water described as 'grossly polluted' has been reduced from 1,278 miles to 952 miles. Substantial improvements have been made in the East Anglian rivers Bure, Yare, Gipping and Orwell. In the Severn basin, the Severn and the Warwickshire Avon are reported as conspicuous successes, and a substantial portion of the tidal Thames has improved significantly. 'Improvement has been due to the steadily increasing expenditure on sewage and trade effluent treatment stimulated by the system of control of discharge to rivers' the survey states.

Much work is required on the Mersey, the Irwell, the Tame, the Tyne, the Tees, the Yorkshire Ouse, the Trent, the Aire and the Bristol Avon.

The stage has been set for the next major advance by the Government proposal that the twenty nine River Authorities of the 1963 Water Resources Act, along with about 1,400 other bodies concerned with water supply, sewerage, etc. should be combined into ten multi-purpose regional authorities. The proposed authorities would have greater powers than the present ones, and when coupled with the large investment announced at the end of 1971, should lead to a great improvement. Legislation for this

Table 3.1

Pollution in non-tidal rivers — England and Wales

Chemical classification	1970		1972		est. 1980	
	miles	%	miles	%	miles	%
					approx.	
Class 1 Unpolluted	17,000	76·2	17.279	77·4	18,100	81
Class 2 Doubtful	3,290	14·7	3,267	14.7	3,350	15
Class 3 Poor	1,071	4·8	939	4·2	670	3
Class 4 Grossly Polluted	952	4·3	832	3·7	199	1
Total England and Wales	22,313	100	22,317	100	22,319	100

change has been introduced, and it could give Britain the most effective machinery of any country in the world for handling water supply and sewage disposal. Practically all the new works will treat sewage at present untreated, or only partly treated before discharge to tidal waters or the sea. In theory, 100 per cent of all sewage discharged to non-tidal rivers is treated to Royal Commission standards (BOD 20 mg/l, S/S 30 mg/l, dilution >8:1), but a number of works are overloaded or inefficient. (The position may be contrasted with that in Germany where only 25 per cent of sewage is treated, and the target of 50 per cent has been set for a five-year programme costing DM.4.5,billion.)

In volume 2 of *River Pollution Survey* 1970 *of England and Wales*, published in July 1972, it was stated that to bring all discharges of sewage and industrial effluent up to the standards that River Authorities expect to impose by 1980 would require an expenditure of about £610 million (1970 prices) for both sewage works and industrial treatment. The forecast improvements for this expenditure are shown in Tables 3.1 and 3.2 along with the 1970 and 1972 data for tidal and non-tidal rivers. A comparison of the 1970 and 1972 figures shows that over the two-year period there has been a reduction in the length of rivers described as poor or grossly polluted by 252 miles in non-tidal rivers and twenty-one miles in tidal rivers. In fact, the grossly polluted regions of tidal rivers have increased by twenty-seven miles, but have been more than made up by the improvements to the poor regions. Looking to the future, if the £610 million improvements are carried out, then those regions described as 'poor' or 'grossly polluted' will amount to 4 per cent for non-tidal rivers, instead of 7·9 per cent as now, and to 15 per cent for tidal rivers instead of 27·4 per cent.

Table 3.2

Pollution in tidal rivers — England and Wales

Chemical classification	1970		1972		est. 1980	
	miles	%	miles	%	miles	%
					approx.	
Class 1 Unpolluted	862	48·1	880	49·4	995	56
Class 2 Doubtful	419	23·4	414	23·2	506	28
Class 3 Poor	301	16·8	253	14·2	223	13
Class 4 Grossly Polluted	209	11·7	236	13·2	59	3
Total England and Wales	1,791	100	1,783	100	1,783	100

Strategy of waste disposal

From the tables and the earlier discussion on resources, it appears that:-

1 There is no shortage of water suitable for supply.
2 The distance water must be transported can be reduced by using un-polluted rivers as conduits.
3 Priority should be given to preserving quality upstream of major con-urbations.
4 Treatment of wastes should be designed to minimise the mass of con-servative anions such as chloride and sulphate, and to reduce nitrates to safe limits for babies. Phosphate removal is not seen to be a necessity. Cations of heavy metals should be removed in treatment plants.
5 Observance of Royal Commission standards for discharges into rivers having more than eight times the flow is needed. For smaller flows, higher standards are needed, or special attention should be given to additional aeration effected naturally, by weirs or mechnical devices.
6 Substandard water, either from pollution or salt incursion, is not gen-erally a source of supply unless Thames water is so regarded. Treatment here is confined to light exposure, followed by filtration of algae, storage in the dark and sterilisation before pumping to mains. This process would need to be used (or some variant) in the case of estuary storage in such regions as the Wash.
7 No suitable economic processes can be put forward now for treatment of brackish waters by such means as ion exchange membranes, reverse osmosis, electrodialysis, etc.
8 Sea-water as a source appears wholly uneconomic whether treatment is as for brackish water, by multiflash distillation, by freezing out clath-rates, or by solar evaporation.

Discussion

Lord Zuckerman: First may I say, Sir Frederick, that I was fascinated by your implied attack on the idea of defining standards in absolute terms. What you said about water pollutants applies to many other fields as well.

Mr D. A. D. Reeve: May I carry on from the point you have just made, Lord Zuckerman, in dealing with one of the matters that sometimes is not appreciated and that is the imprecise nature of the sewage treatment process. Even with a well designed works working within its capacity the results achieved show substantial variations. We have been talking about the

Royal Commission effluent standard. One has only to say that in order to achieve 95 per cent compliance, which is a high level of compliance, with the Royal Commission standard of 20 mg/l for BOD, one has to achieve an average of about 11 mg/l, and to achieve about 80 per cent compliance with the standard, one has to achieve an average of about 13 mg/l. This means, of course, that any treatment plant producing a Royal Commission effluent will be producing, on average, something like 13 mg/l of BOD, which, in the case of those authorities discharging into streams with very low dilution factors, means that a grossly polluted river level BOD of 12 is perpetuated. Where the dilution factor is high, discharges of Royal Commission standard can be made without the quality of the river being moved from one category into a worse category. In the industrial Midlands where some of the rivers are 95 per cent sewage effluent and where the major rivers are 50 per cent sewage effluent, one has to look very carefully at the effect of Royal Commission standards and one has to do very much better than this in order to enable a stream to be moved out of the grossly polluted river category.

The West Midlands is an industrial area and the sewers do bring in large quantities of trade effluents up to about one-third of the total flow, and this does, of course, produce serious problems of trade effluent control. Although trade effluent control is an essential requirement, even here there are occasions when the exclusion of certain trade effluents adversely affect the treatment process; the presence of iron in sewage for example may materially help the settlement process although it may adversely affect the subsequent biochemical processes. One hopes to fix the consents to discharge industrial effluents at such a level that their compliance with them is not too onerous, but clearly, control must be stringent enough to ensure that the standard of treatment and the quality of effluents are not adversely affected.

The problem of trade effluents and the Deposit of Poisonous Waste Act is really one and the same problem, I think. I have no doubt that some of the toxic wastes that arrive at sewage treatment works are the result of gaps in trade effluent control, and there is some little evidence – and I would not want to stress this – that since the introduction of the Deposit of Poisonous Waste Act there has been a rather higher level of contravention of trade effluent control concept than was previously the case. I think the two are very closely related and one does wonder whether the responsibility for the Deposit of Poisonous Waste Act should still remain with local authorities.

It has to be realised that every sewage works manager accepts material for processing without knowing its constituents except in the very broadest terms, and similarly, every sewage works manager discharges effluents which may contain constituents of which he is unaware both quantitatively and qualitatively. This is broadly the situation in every sewage treatment works in the country except in respect of the two parameters which everybody measures — suspended solids and the biochemical oxygen demand. There is no doubt at all that with the passage of time one will have to seek to do very much more monitoring of the sewage and the effluents discharged from the works and to make very much more strenuous efforts to determine those materials which may have subsequent effects upon the process itself and the rivers into which effluents discharge.

Lord Zuckerman: Do you anticipate any difficulty in providing for a greater degree of monitoring?

Mr D. A. D. Reeve: There are no suitable tools. This is a very major difficulty.

Sir Frederick Warner: This is important as regards small treatment works. Suspended solids and biochemical oxygen are not the only things, and these are not the only limits set in the consent to discharge; it will set out all the other materials and the permitted amounts and concentrations. The monitoring is difficult, but we are almost in a condition now where we have too many aids to monitoring.

I do want to know what is coming down, particularly in the way of formaldehyde or anything which is going to alter the microbiological population of the sewage works. These are the really important things one needs to know about, and it is a problem for small sewage treatment works. The difficulty does not exist at the very large ones. One of the odd things which arose out of the vision of the Victorian engineers in building these very big cut-off sewers is that they act as huge chemical reactors and by the time it gets to the treatment works practically everything has been reacted and one does not have to do anything about it. Therefore the limits set by the Greater London Council for discharge are much more lenient than is the case with any other authority in the country.

Mr D. A. D. Reeve: May I say on that that I think it is important to know what one is doing, and at the present moment one makes analyses of effluents for two reasons, first, to try to assess the effect on the river, and secondly, to try to assess the way one is operating one's plant. The only way of looking at this on an instantaneous basis is to take a bottle, to look at it, and to say that if it is near enough like gin it is alright. The BOD test takes six days before you get the results back.

Lord Zuckerman: Six days to do a BOD test — the National Health Service can do better than that with blood serum ... a few hours to identify and measure a dozen parameters.

50

Mr J. McLoughlin: Sir Frederick Warner mentioned the charges scheme that is being proposed. I do not know whether all the consequences of such a scheme have been considered. When someone releases pollutants into a river it often results in persons downstream suffering damage. If the public authority collects a charge, the money would appear to go into the wrong pockets — the public authority receives it while the man downstream suffers the resulting damage.

It would be possible to permit the riparian owner who suffers to make a claim against the fund into which the charges are paid. You would then have to decide whether or not he would lose his right to apply for an injunction. If he did, the charges scheme would involve a compulsory purchase of his present Common Law rights.

If he were not permitted to claim against the fund, presumably his Common Law rights would remain intact. In the event of his exercising them the discharger might justly complain that he was compelled to pay twice — once to the public authority and then to the riparian owner. I am assuming, of course, that although there will be some response to the charge it will not be total, for the scheme does envisage the payment of some charge.

Lord Zuckerman: The scheme also envisages the payment of a smaller charge the cleaner the effluent that is put in. The assumption was that everybody had to have a licence to put effluent into a sewer. We wanted to see the licence system extended and the charge to be reduced the cleaner the material that is put in. This is something that is beginning to happen in the USA, and I am sure that Dr Russell could tell us more about it. We were quite clear in our own minds what we wanted. We did not imagine that we would be passing on charges or burdens to people downstream who were going to be affected by pollutants added upstream.

Mr J. McLoughlin: In many streches of river more stringent and careful control will be necessary in the future even to maintain the present quality of the river water. Insufficient attention has been paid to the techniques of control by legal measures. We are still somewhat in the 'horse and buggy' days in this respect.

River Authorities have legal powers simply to grant licences to discharge into rivers. To exercise this form of control effectively they obviously need fairly comprehensive monitoring. I have no doubt that in certain key stretches of river there is some continuous monitoring, but in many large stretches there are checks on discharges no oftener than once per month — once per year in some cases. So far as flow rates are concerned, on the information I have from River Authorities, flow meters are installed for a relatively few large discharges.

Admittedly the River Authorities are checking also on river quality, at over 500 points in some Authority areas, but again the checks are usually only once per month. All this is inadequate for really effective enforcement. The River Authorities themselves are not to blame, for they are subject to two limitations. One is that they cannot legally impose upon firms conditions as to treatment before they discharge their effluents. The other is that they cannot attach to a consent a condition that the discharger should monitor his own discharge.

Despite these limitations they do attempt to enforce their consent conditions. In this process many River Authorities prefer to use persuasion rather than coercion to achieve permanent improvement. The resulting enforcement is far from rigorous. As part of a questionnaire, in 1971, I asked River Authorities how many dischargers regularly exceeded their consent levels, 'regularly' being defined as on over 50 per cent of occasions when checks were made or the facts otherwise known. The replies I received related to dischargers. Of the sixteen Authorities replying ten said that of dischargers 20 per cent regularly exceeded consent levels, and for some the percentage was considerably higher. In one Authority the figure was 60 per cent for all dischargers and 72 per cent if industrial dischargers alone were considered. If we then look at the number of prosecutions, we find that in 1970 there were sixty-four proceedings brought under the Acts, leading to fifty-seven convictions and in 1971, sixty-seven prosecutions and fifty-eight convictions.

These figures show that the registers of consents kept by River Authorities are in many cases misleading. They also suggest that better techniques are needed for the proper enforcement of consent conditions. Some River Authorities have in fact tried to use a different technique to improve the quality of discharges into their rivers. Instead of merely watching the discharges, they have tried to put pressure on firms to adopt better methods of treatment. This is a sound approach, because obviously if you can pressure for technological progress on firms you are going to achieve some permanent improvement. The Alkali Inspectorate uses this method successfully in controlling discharges to and from scheduled processes. But to use it successfully, men of the right qualifications and experience are needed, and this is where, through no fault of their own, River Authorities fall short.

What we need is a thorough review of the techniques of control which could be made available to pollution control authorities. In the case of water pollution we need not be restricted to watching the end of a pipeline.

In my submission pollution control begins with land use planning. By a

52

judicious use of the powers at their disposal, local planning authorities can reduce considerably the problems which would otherwise face the pollution control authorities. They have in recent years become more conscious of this, and since 1968 they have been required, in drawing up their structure plans, to have regard to the improvement of the physical environment. In my submission they could also usefully act as co-ordinating authorities between the various pollution control bodies when developments are being planned.

From the point of view of river pollution, the present system of planning control does not always work satisfactorily. Planning authorities are able to delegate powers to small district councils, many of which are anxious to attract development to their areas, and will do so at the expense of seriously increased pollution. And with councils responding differently to River Authority requests, there can be an uneven patchwork of development.

May I suggest a simple reform to our planning law which would provide a useful aid to pollution control. This would be to require anyone applying under the Town and Country Planning Act for consent to develop land to make a simple statement of the wastes which will be discharged from that development. In particular cases the River Authority could then make representations, and in total the information would be most useful to all authorities concerned with the disposal of wastes. The planning authority itself could attach conditions to its consent, limiting the amount of waste to be discharged to the figures in the application. Too often, at a public enquiry into a planning application, have figures been given which have been considerably exceeded within a few years of the consent being granted.

After planning consent has been given, pollution control can be applied at a number of successive stages. If you look at any process which creates pollution, you will usually find that the farther back along the line you go the easier control becomes. In the first place controls could be applied to the processes used or the products distributed. We have them already in the voluntary scheme governing the production of detergents for household use, and this has improved rivers considerably. Reference has been made in this discussion to pollutants damaging to human health. As these are identified we may find that in some cases the best safeguard is to apply control at the point of production where it is much easier to enforce. I understand also that there are proposals that people using containers for storing poisonous substances sited near rivers will have to comply with regulations which will be issued by the Secretary of State. These will fall into the same category, and again there should be no difficulty in enforcement.

The next stage of control is at the treatment of waste before discharge. If the Regional Water Authorities (RWAs) are given powers to require a firm to use a certain type of treatment of waste before discharge, and if they are given men of the right qualifications and experience, this will obviate a great deal of the inspection that now has to be carried out and is so expensive. This method is already used by the Alkali Inspectorate for discharges to air, and is applied to discharges to water by authorities in the USA and Canada.

Lastly there is control of discharges through the pipe-line. 'Watching the end of a pipe-line' is a very time-consuming and expensive operation, but if we are to have really effective protection for rivers it may be necessary. In that case there appears to be no logical reason why, in appropriate cases, the discharger himself should not be required to install, at his own expence, approved equipment for measuring the flow and perhaps taking samples or automatically monitoring quality. This requirement is already imposed by other authorities in this country. The users of certain furnaces can be required to measure grit and dust, and if an industrial firm seeks to discharge into a sewer the local authority may require monitoring equipment to be installed at the firm's expense. There seems to be ample justification for the RWAs doing the same, and thus transferring the cost of monitoring from the public purse to the discharger himself.

There is thus a whole armoury of weapons available in the legal arsenal to combat pollution. If we are to have effective control, giving adequate protection of rivers, we must equip the RWAs with a far wider range of powers which they can exercise at their discretion in appropriate cases.

Mr S. V. Ellis: I am wondering what you will do if you take samples every day. Who will process them? What will it cost, and what will it be worth in the long run? Perhaps I am rather naïve on this, because we have fairly clean rivers in my authority and we do not get these industrial problems. We know by and large what is going into our rivers. Most of our industry is allied to the agricultural industry, but we know over a period what sort of effluent they are discharging. They are not likely one day unless there has been an accident, to put something in the river that we do not know about. And even if we were doing more sampling than, say, once a month, it would be by no means certain that we would be there on that particular day.

I am talking about a rural area, but most pollution officers of River Authorities know what is coming from their industrial concerns. They know the type of effluent, and I am not sure that very frequent sampling would advance the cause of the prevention of pollution very much.

54

What I do say is that I think River Authorities should use their powers of prosecution perhaps more than they do. I was alarmed the other week to hear two of my colleagues say that they did not believe in prosecution but in persuasion. I do not, not now; perhaps I did in 1952. In those early days we tried to persuade people and local industries. They said, 'We will leave you and go to Grimsby; we are not going to put in pollution plant – we cannot afford to do so'. Eventually, when I took out a summons, they had the plant put in very quickly – and they are still with us. We are now top of the league on clean rivers, and we had honourable mention in the first report for having achieved great improvements. I recall that somebody said that there is nothing that clarifies the mind like an impending execution. That has been our experience.

The other problem is keeping local authorities up to scratch. I wonder how we are going to do this. At the moment one gets a bad report; one writes to the town clerk; he reprimands the sewage works manager, and one gets an immediate improvement. In future I understand we are going to have, for the first three years at any rate, management units. I do not know who I am going to write to if the effluent from a sewage works is not up to standard, or who is going to see that something is done. This is one of the things that I would like to find out. We have, for instance, a case now where a local authority has accepted a trade effluent which has put the sewage works completely out of focus. We prosecuted them and they were fined £50. It took them about three weeks before they decided to stop this particular firm from putting this stuff down the sewer. The firm are putting it on the land; when the land is saturated it goes back into the river – and I do not know what will happen. They have been so tardy in even doing that that we have said that we will prosecute them again. I think this is by far the easier way to tackle these matters.

I am not at all sure that we want River Authority staffs to advise industry as to how it should treat its effluent. I think that industry can well afford to employ its own experts to do this. I think that the River Authority must say standard it requires for a river, and it should be up to industry to see that it complies with that standard.

On the point about powers for a River Authority to say what sort of treatment there should be, we have had only a limited experiment with the extended aeration units for small housing estates which nevertheless were a terrible nuisance to everybody concerned unless they had adequate maintenance for twenty-four hours a day seven days of the week. In our conditions of consent we tried to say that these things should not be used, or, if they were, the local authority must take them over, but unfortunately we lost on appeal. The Minister said that the powers of consent

55

under the 1951 Act did not give us power to say that. I think that in certain conditions this might be a very useful provision. However, these things are going slightly out of favour, so that the problem does not now arise in the same way that it did.

On monitoring, we insist where there are big discharges, on having a meter. I do not know what use chemical monitoring would be so far as we are concerned. If you are going to use powers of prosecution, how do you prosecute a man on his own records.

Mr G. W. Curtis: The thing that really worries me about the whole business is that I doubt very much whether adequate expertise exist at the grass roots level. This is one of the major problems of the new Regional Water Authorities, and that is why I wholeheartedly welcome them.

I was surprised and a little disappointed when I heard Sir Frederick rather condone the standard of sewage effluents on suspended solids and *BOD*. I have been building sewage works for thirty years, and I seem to design them on the same parameters as I did when I started. I would have thought we ought to be getting away from this and moving on a lot further. Most of those here are concerned with the larger problems of London and Birmingham but I know some of the results in this area of Norfolk of using this standard as the gospel; I call it the Ministry's 'Little Red Book', because if one designs any scheme which will meet this standard one will get automatic approval. I know that some of these schemes produce results that really are wasteful in terms of local conditions and circumstances. In other cases they produce damaging results because of the effects on ecology. In some cases they are positively dangerous. I know that one reads 'The chairman opened the sewage works and drank the effluent'. I know a lot of chairmen I would like to see do that! I am currently engaged in a contest over the building of some sea outfalls. People say that there must be treatment, but what does sewage treatment mean based on these standards of suspended solids and BOD. They mean absolutely nothing.

It has been said that we cannot define pollution in absolute standards and terms. I accept this. What I still hope is that if the Regional Water Authorities are large enough, and powerful enough, and attract the right expertise, biological, chemical and engineering, to establish specific standards for specific conditions, then we could move away from BOD and suspended solids and have a specific condition for each river having regard to the function which that river is supposed to perform.

I would like to say a quick word on industrial waste. I was interested to hear Sir Frederick Warner say that industrial wastes are not the real trouble. I can assure him that they are the trouble in rural areas where you have small works from which the relative proportions of effluent are considerable. It disturbs me greatly that the charge imposed on the acceptance of industrial waste by a local authority is again based on the suspended solids and BOD figure. Although in some cases one does list constituents which may not be discharged, this is not done in all cases; it is certainly not monitored and it is not done with the amount of expertise that it ought to be. This is the sort of expertise that I hope will be vested in the new Regional Water Authorities.

One of the results of increased action on industrial wastes will be industrial dumping. We have already had some of this at one place in Norfolk. As a result of the work of the Royal Commission, we have got the new Toxic Wastes Act. This is a good Act, but I wish that it were a little stronger. I wish there was a responsibility on the depositor to prove that where he is going to deposit is safe, rather than the other way round. One of the results of stepping up the control of industrial waste and controlling tipping may well be the building and development of treatment complexes by industry. We have had one projected in Norfolk, by an international firm, which would cost half a million pounds. It looks like being refused on planning grounds which is really very distressing. It is a pity that toxic waste dosposal and dumping is not within the control of the Regional Water Authorities.

I think it is also a pity that one could not have the control, and the whole chemical, biological and engineering expertise in one powerful unit. There is the same type of difficulty in the new Bill in which the Ministry is obviously being politically pressurised into giving the sewerage functions to the district councils. I do not see how you can control a sewage without controlling the material that comes into it. I know that this is a political necessity in order to get the Bill through but nevertheless it is a tragedy. I would have liked to see the Regional Water Authority as a very powerful authority with tremendous expertise, the sort of authority which could say what is the standard for a particular river, with the engineering skill to convert that into practice, and with sufficient expertise to proclaim with authority on the effects and dangers of tipping and dumping which constitute some of the biggest risks to the water supply of this country.

Mr B. R. Thorpe: I follow Mr Curtis in expressing the hope that the Regional Water Authorities will be to some extent our answer, not only because, they have the possibility of attracting the right staff, but because possibly, for the first time, they have the opportunity of creating the right atmosphere. None of us who have worked for local authorities have failed to see the annual stampede at budget time. Sewage disposal is always the last item to be considered for inclusion in the estimates, and it is always the first to be considered for exclusion, for the very simple reason that very often the local authority, by spending money in that direction, is merely improving the lot of the people further down the river. That is not its first priority when looking at an overburdened budget.

While the enforcement and setting of standards is important. I think much the most important ingredient is setting the right atmosphere and creating an incentive to the authority to cleanse its water, in the hope that it can re-sell it. This is the sort of motivation that will create long-term benefits and which all the controls in the world will never ensure.

Dr R. G. Allen: To refer back to Sir Frederick Warner's earlier remarks, I would like to make the point that the rivers to which he referred present some very serious problems from the water supply point of view. He knows a great deal about the Thames, but the Seine, for instance, is very different. Abstractions from the Seine have to be elaborately treated. Even powerful oxidisation processes have to be employed to make the water drinkable. It may be that Sir Frederick was relying mainly upon his experience on the Thames, which is unique, and not necessarily respresentative of the United Kingdom as a whole, in saying that be believes that all is well. I do not believe it is.

I would also suggest that Sir Frederick left out a most important aspect when he was talking about oxygen. All the 'dirty water' people will refer first to BOD, but water supply people are most interested in the materials in water that do not degrade, and these are definitely on the increase. This indicates that the Royal Commission standard which was put in the days when industrial effluents were so very different is now irrelevant as a quality standard. As was already stated, it is still of value for controlling the performance of the sewage works. I welcome Mr Curtis's remark that we have to start thinking of a new standard which reflects these important aspects of non-gradable materials.

Sir Frederick Warner: I said that I stood by the Royal Commission standard because if you take it in this context it represents what I think you need, which is a mass balance. With regard to the other rivers, of course they do not have sewage treatment of the material which is discharged into them. That is why they have difficulties in water supply.

Sir Norman Rowntree: In the table in his paper Sir Frederick described Class 1 as unpolluted. This is the description in the river water quality survey recently produced, but from the water supply point of view those rivers should be stated as no more than good. Most of them are certainly polluted, and thus unpolluted is a misleading description.

Dr A. L. Downing: I would like to say a word about the non-degradable fraction of sewage effluent. Determination of its composition presents a reasonably formidable problem in analysis. Regrettably about 30 per cent has so far been identified. However research is in progress and the present position is indicated in Table 3.3. The total content of non-degradable soluble organic carbon in a good effluent is about 20 mg/1. About 95 per cent has been roughly characterised in terms of general groupings. To characterise these in terms of specific substances one has to use the most sophisticated analytical tools. From work done over the past eighteen months only about 30 per cent has been so identified.

Perhaps the main point to make is that one finds substances which were probably not in purely domestic sewage effluent say ten or fifteen years ago. Some are steroids, some organo-chlorines, and some substances such as optical brighteners. With modern methods of analysis one can find substances at extremely low concentrations. For example, optical brighteners can be measured down to concentrations of 10^{-12} g/l. Clearly the significance of the presence of any material at a concentration as low as this seems questionable. Some forty-seven substances have been identified so far, and as analytical tools are refined probably hundreds more will be found. Many may well be dangerous if ingested in the quantities in which one takes normal food but they are present in such minute amounts in effluents that it is unrealistic to imagine them as hazards. However, by developing this background of knowledge about substances normally present one can establish the levels which appear to be safe by virtue of lack of correlation between differences in concentration drunk by different populations and incidence of disease. Then one can go on to detect changes in the prevailing levels or the presence of new substances and arrange to get physiological tests, perhaps tests on experimental animals done, or analyses of that kind.

Mr V. K. Collinge: May I make one point in relation to Sir Frederick Warner's introduction when he challenged my previous assertion that we need to know a great deal more about what we drink and what is safe and what is not safe. Dr Downing's contribution is relevant to this, but Sir Frederick also mentioned that fish were susceptible to heavy metals at varying concentrations, the degree of effect depending on the hardness of the water. When I previously referred to cardio-vascular disease I was careful to say that the evidence was statistical and the point is that it might not be the hardness which is causing the problem. It might be a question of the association of hardness with copper or with phenols, or something like that. I think this underlines the need for us to get to the root of the effects of these substances on the human body.

Lord Zuckerman: I think Dr Downing was correct when he pointed out

Table 3.3

Identification of soluble organic constituents of effluent from full biological treatment of domestic sewage

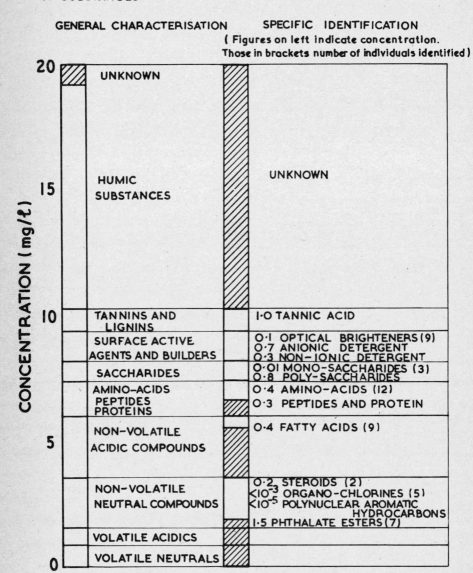

TOTAL CONCENTRATION SPECIFICALLY IDENTIFIED 6·2 mg/ℓ COMPRISING 47 SUBSTANCES

GENERAL CHARACTERISATION / SPECIFIC IDENTIFICATION
(Figures on left indicate concentration. Those in brackets number of individuals identified)

CONCENTRATION (mg/ℓ)

General Characterisation	Specific Identification
UNKNOWN	
HUMIC SUBSTANCES	UNKNOWN
TANNINS AND LIGNINS	1·0 TANNIC ACID
SURFACE ACTIVE AGENTS AND BUILDERS	0·1 OPTICAL BRIGHTENERS (9) 0·7 ANIONIC DETERGENT 0·3 NON−IONIC DETERGENT
SACCHARIDES	0·01 MONO−SACCHARIDES (3) 0·8 POLY−SACCHARIDES
AMINO−ACIDS PEPTIDES PROTEINS	0·4 AMINO−ACIDS (12) 0·3 PEPTIDES AND PROTEIN
NON−VOLATILE ACIDIC COMPOUNDS	0·4 FATTY ACIDS (9)
NON−VOLATILE NEUTRAL COMPOUNDS	0·2 STEROIDS (2) $<10^{-3}$ ORGANO−CHLORINES (5) $<10^{-5}$ POLYNUCLEAR AROMATIC HYDROCARBONS 1·5 PHTHALATE ESTERS (7)
VOLATILE ACIDICS	
VOLATILE NEUTRALS	

that with modern methods of detection and measurement one can pick up hundreds of substances. I should be surprised if by the time you have dealt with the other 70 per cent you do find, not hundreds, but thousands of substances. This brings us back to the question of standards. I certainly accept what Sir Frederick said about the unreality of setting rigid standards regardless of circumstances. There are two alternative methods of dealing with this problem. You can either have the codex method which specifies what things are allowed; or you can specify what is disallowed. The latter is the method we have followed in this country, although it is not that of other countries. The problem is epitomised in the USA by the Delaney Amendment to the Food and Drugs Act, which disallows any substance which can be shown to be carcinogenic, whatever the circumstances. This means that in setting standards in the USA one has to prove a negative when it comes to food additives, drugs, or environmental pollutions. I am therefore nervous about the possibility that we will start discovering trace-amounts of substances, not because of the pleasure of knowing that they are there, but because of the danger that this will lead to the imposition of even more standards based upon the proposition that one can prove negatives.

I think that the legal problems that have been discussed, the various sanctions, are not the critical issue. What is critical is the monitoring. We must have better monitoring, and we have to know what it is that we need to monitor.

Sir Norman Rowntree: We ought to know why we are monitoring and what we want the river to do. I do not like the use of the word 'standards'. Standard implies the same criteria throughout the country for every river and effluent and that may not be necessary or desirable.

Mr R. C. Chilver: One thing that we want a standard for is what the human frame is to drink. The human frame is the same throughout the country. I thought it was quite reasonable that the Chief Medical Officer of Health in Whitehall should guide the people who supply water for drinking purposes about what they should test for and complain about. Then it seems to me that the problem of effluent falls into place. Once you make the same public body responsible for controlling all effluents and the supply of drinking water, that multi-purpose authority can say, 'I will accept a very dirty effluent and spend a lot of money on treating it for drinking', or it can say, 'I will keep my water treatment works to a minimum and put up the cost of treatment of effluent'. But you do not on that basis need a uniform standard for your effluents because your control is exercised over the clean water.

Sir Norman Rowntree: The body responsible for the quality of the river for other than drinking water purposes — the recreational and amenity — should also state what it requires.

Mr J. E. Beddoe: We have a Water Quality Steering Committee which is trying to devise water quality guidelines which will take account of the use of a particular stretch of river.

Sir Frederick Warner: This is a reinforcement of what Sir Norman said about the relevance of the purpose of the river.

Dr R. G. Allen: When the Regional Water Authorities are functioning we will know what compromises and optimisations are reached as between dirty and clean. When public health is at stake, what compromises and economies are made on the treatment of the effluent as opposed to the cleaning up of the abstraction? Standards may have to play a part.

On the cardio-vascular situation, it could well be that the real relationship is with copper, but the interesting thing is that we do not monitor for copper although we do monitor for hardness. When the medical people look for a correlation, the only data they find is on hardness, and they have to do with that.

Dr A. L. Downing: On the question of the failure to reach standards, of course it is not failure of technical understanding. Although I do not condone these failures I think it is rather easy to over-estimate their significance. It is not that on the one side you have right and on the other side wrong. It is often the difference between achieving perhaps 92 per cent and, say, 90 per cent purification. The failure are not, generally speaking, all that dramatic. There is really no problem in getting it right from the technical point of view. It is usually a question of the community being prepared to will a bit more money.

Mr Eldon Griffiths: Whenever I have attended these seminars in East Anglia I have departed thinking that I knew what ought to be done and I have arrived at the House of Commons and discovered what can be done. One has to try to relate the second to the first.

I would like to comment, as a layman, on some of the matters already raised and then perhaps say one or two things about the feasibility of legislation.

I was particularly struck by Dr Allen's comments about the increasing irrelevance of the Royal Commission standard, a view that Sir Frederick Warner did not entirely share; but if it is a fact that the Royal Commission standard in no way provides a measure for the non-degradables, which are increasing, then I think that probably we shall have to have a look at this. I will obviously get some advice on it.

The particular point that Mr Curtis made was that the critical shortage may well be of expertise. I have no doubt that by putting things together within the Regional Water Authorities we will make better use of the expertise we have, but I beg leave to doubt whether we have actually got enough in the country anyway. I was particularly interested to hear Mr Curtis say that the would have liked to see waste disposal, the whole tipping control, brought within the general ambit of the Regional Water Authorities. Of course, if you start an all-purpose authority you can ultimately control everything. One might allege, to some extent, that pollution arises from motor vehicles, but one could not slip them in as well. But I do take the point made. I think that when the new county councils take over and establish a more intelligent strategy for the disposal of wastes, pulverising and so on, the closest possible links between the County Authorities and the Regional Water Authorities will be indispensable.

I would like also to comment very briefly on Mr Ellis's remarks. I was very glad to hear that he is a 'prosecutor'. In the alkali field I think that persuasion has generally worked best and I think persuasion is certainly the way in which governments would always prefer to go; but from time to time nailing an exemplary prosecution on the wall so that everybody can see it does a power of good. Unfortunately, as things now stand, the fines frequently imposed are quite derisory. That is why we shall need to bring in legislation to increase the levels of fine for all forms of pollution offence.

Mr Thorpe rightly pinpointed that the important thing is to create not just the machinery but the right atmosphere, and the phrase that he used − that there should be an atmosphere in which an authority would cleanse its water in the hope that it could resell it − was absolutely correct and is very much the spirit of what the Bill intends to achieve.

I would like to say a word about the National Water Council. Obviously the main things it has to do are: first, to provide the Secretary of State with advice on national water strategy in the widest sense of the word, and secondly, to promote and assist the Regional Water Authorities in the efficient performance of their duties. The Council will be the source of type approval for taps and pipes and fittings. It will be the main body responsible for training, and it will also be responsible for ensuring that proper wage negotiating machinery is created. It will, have to be the main source of advice to the Secretary of State and the water authorities themselves on the structure of charging. It will be for each RWA to make its charges in terms of its own situation, its own financial and other constraints, but I think there must be a consistent structures of charges across the whole country, and it is here that the National Water Council will play a special role.

The other thing that I want to convey is what it is proposed to do about planning and research. I know there has been concern about this. I think the first concern is that there must be a central planning capability, and secondly that we must use this possibly unique opportunity to tidy up the overlapping and duplication that there has been in the research field. It is planned that there will be three new bodies. One of them will be a Central Water Planning Unit, the second a Water Research Centre, and the third, much smaller, a Data Collection Unit.

The primary task of the Central Water Planning Unit, will be to study and advise on all the major strategic options, to advise the Secretary of State, the National Water Council and, through them, the Regional Water Authorities. It will be drawn mainly from the planning divisions of the Water Resources Board (WRB), and they should remain largely intact within it. It will be centred at Reading and will be run by the Steering Committee of the National Water Council, the Water Research Centre, and the Government. The Central Water Planning Unit, under a chairman appointed by the Secretary of State, will continue to provide a central planning capability for water strategy.

The Water Reasearch Centre will be a new body, though in the form of a research association. What we have in mind is to bring together the Water Research Association (WRA) the technology divisions of the Water Resources Board, and the Water Pollution Research Laboratory, and most probably about two-thirds of the research and development on water services that is generated by our own Department of the Environment Directorate of Water Engineering. The Government will be putting in two-thirds of the Directorate of Water Engineering's effort. This means that all or most of the major research capabilities will be drawn together from the department, from WPRL, from WRB, and from industry represented by the WRA. The new Research Centre will have a small council to guide it. As an idea of the scale, at the moment the amount of research is about £2½ million spread very widely. We hope that this new Water Research Centre will in a few years time command a budget of about £4 million a year and operate in a much more effective manner.

Finally, there is the Data Collection Unit. I think this speaks for itself. A relatively small body, it will reside primarily within the Department of the Environment. However, all of these groups, the planning, the research, the data collection, must of course fit well together and dovetail with the National Water Council.

I am grateful for the invitation to be here, I have been impressed by what I have heard. Then we get the bill you will have to make it work.

Dr J. Rees: May I ask where the economic research is going to be done. It does not seem to fit in with the basic physical science research at the

Water Research Centre and would be more appropriately linked to the planning services.

Mr Eldon Griffiths: The answer, shortly, is that I do not know.

Mr J. E. Beddoe: There will be some in the Central Water Planning Unit. However, I think Dr Rees is implicitly asking about research into the form of charges and tariff structures, on which work has just started. This research will have to be developed by the National Water Council and the Department, since these issues will be important to the success of Regional Water Authorities. The problems are difficult and will not be solved quickly.

Dr R. G. Allen: It may not be easy to attract £4 million from this new industry. It will have to make good about £1 million formerly provided from DOE, £$\frac{1}{2}$ million from WRB, and £$\frac{3}{4}$ million from WPRL, and it must take time to get people to agree that this is a worthwhile investment. I think we have managed to do it on the clean water side, but on the dirty water side it has never had to be done.

Mr Eldon Griffiths: I said that I thought it would build up in a few years time to that figure. It is not in any way an unreasonable figure when you consider what a big industry this is. There is something like £400 million a year capital investment. If you take the dirty water side – I realise most of it is in civil engineering – £800 million is going into new sewage service. Given the input from that, to ask the industry to raise the rest is not asking very much of it.

Professor P. O. Wolf: We are in a university. Do the universities fit in at all? There was no mention of their research capabilities and educational capabilities, although there was a specific reference to training in connection with the National Water Council.

Mr Eldon Griffiths: The new Water Research Centre will contract out a great deal of work. It will not have all that much in-house capability in some fields. I would have thought that it would have to come to the appropriate university to do the job.

I should perhaps add that of course we have got to work very closely with our colleagues in Europe on a lot of this. I accept that our circumstances are different. We are an island, we have not quite the same environmental background, and I am rather with those who have said that one should avoid absolute standards. But we ought to work with Europe in quite a lot of things, and particularly in research. Already under the CCMS wing of NATO we have gone into some very good work with Germany and the USA on new forms of sewage technology. I suspect that on water quality we shall want to obtain the information of other countries and make our information available to them. One of the things I shall be saying in Brussels is that we are very happy to share such knowledge as we have on mathematical modelling and some of the water pollution research. We would expect within the EEC a common shared exchange. I think the universities all over Europe, including this country, have an important part to play.

4   Restraining Demand

Dr C. S. RUSSELL

The theoretical case for the pricing of water supplies and waste water disposal is, it seems to me, sufficiently well known and established to require nothing but the briefest of restatements.[1] Water is similar to nearly every other good purchased by consumers and producers in that an extra unit is valued less highly as the quantity (per unit time) purchased increases. That is, the typical consumer's demand curve slopes down to the right, and hence, so does the aggregate curve for a group of consumers. Or, as Samuelson has more vividly put it:[2]

> When water is very dear, I demand only enough of it to drink. Then when its price drops, I buy some to wash with. At still lower prices, I resort to still other uses; finally, when it is really very cheap, I water flowers and use it lavishly for any possible purpose.

The question it seems that this seminar must consider is whether the theoretical arguments have practical merit; whether the pricing of water supplies and waste water disposal can, in fact, make a significant difference in quantities demanded at a particular time, and whether, over the longer run, pricing can affect the rate of growth of demand and hence the need for capacity expanding investments on the part of water suppliers. I shall, therefore, review some of the empirical work on these issues which has been done in the United States. To anticipate the conclusions suggested by this research and to provide a focus for the discussion, let me make the following five points:

1   There appears to be conclusive evidence that demand curves for water withdrawals are, in fact, significantly elastic—both for industrial and some domestic uses.[3]
2   The elasticity of demand varies with the category of use involved, but for some categories of domestic use it is much greater than one in absolute value.
3   There is also evidence that pricing policies can affect the growth of demand over time in such a way that additions to system capacity can be delayed or reduced in size.
4   The response of residuals dischargers to effluent charges or sewer-sys-

tem service charges is less well documented, but such research results as have been reported point to the conclusion that a system of such charges can have a large impact on quantities of residuals discharged, particularly from industrial water users.

5   Taken together, the evidence seems to me to argue very strongly for the use of water abstraction pricing and effluent (or sewer service) charges in any integrated river basin management scheme where water quantity and quality are scarce resources.

The discussion which follows will be divided for convenience into four sections: (a) the impact of metering (or the institution of a non-zero price); (b) estimates of demand curves; (c) pricing and the time path of system expansion; and (d) effluent (or sewer service) charges. In reviewing research under headings, I make no claims to completeness. I have tried, instead, to concentrate on the best work that has come to my attention.[4]

The impact of metering

The simplest question one can ask about water pricing is: What difference does it make to have a non-zero as opposed to a zero price (a flat rate)? That is, what difference does metering and unit pricing make, on average over a range of prices? The most straightforward answer is to reproduce the now famous table from the classic Howe and Linaweaver article.[5] There is a difference and, not surprisingly, that difference is found in use for lawn sprinkling, the use least closely connected to the fundamental concerns of cooking, drinking and sanitation. In metered areas, average sprinkling use is about 44 per cent of that in flat-rate areas. Measured against potential evapotranspiration, the lavish use of water in the flat-rate areas is even more obvious. The ratios of summer sprinkling to summer PTE are 0·6 for the metered areas and 1.8 for the flat-rate areas. There is no significant difference between the areas in the quantity of household water used (i.e. water for cooking, washing, drinking, flushing).[6]

It is perhaps worth noting that the Howe-Linaweaver article, which will be used again below, is based on the data from a very ambitious research project conducted by Johns Hopkins University during the 1960s in a number of areas of the United States, with the support of the Federal Housing Administration. The reports from this project contain a mine of information on water use, but they have become extraordinarily scarce. I provide here a list of the major reports, as they may be of interest.

F. P. Linaweaver Jr, *Final and Summary Report on the Residential Water Use Research Project*, July 1966.

F. P. Linaweaver Jr. John C. Geyer, and Jerome B. Wolff, *Final and Summary Report on Phase Two*, Department of Environmental Engineering Science, Johns Hopkins University, June 1966.

F. P. Linaweaver Jr. James C. Beebe, and Frank A. Skrivan, *Data Report of the Residential Water Use Research Project*, Johns Hopkins University, Department of Environmental Engineering Science, Baltimore, June 1966.

Jerome B. Wolff, F. P. Linaweaver Jr, and John C. Geyer, *Water Used in Selected Commercial and Institutional Establishments in the Baltimore Metropolitan Area*, Johns Hopkins University, June 1966.

Other sources of data on this question include: the compendium *Modern Water Rates*,[7] an article in *American City Magazine*,[8] and a paper by Hanke.[9]

Estimates of demand curves for water withdrawals

There has been considerable work (albeit of widely varying quality) done on the estimation of demand curves for water withdrawals. In Table 4.2, I summarise the results of some of this work by showing the estimates of demand elasticities reported for municipal demand as an undifferentiated aggregate.[10] Notice that these authors report quite a range of results for price elasticities, probably indicating that different mixes of demand types, are represented in their data. Since several of the lower estimates are close to zero and since only the two highest are greater than one, can this table be taken as evidence of 'significant' demand price elasticity? To answer this question, it is necessary to observe that the alternative hypothesis, favoured by many in the water supply field, is that demand is zero elastic; i.e. that water, in the quantities normally used by customers of municipal water systems, is a 'requirement'. In this context, I do think the table indicates significant elasticity, though clearly the bulk of municipal water use is hardly in the luxury category (price elasticity greater than one).

But for further detail on this question, let us turn to the Howe-Linaweaver paper which contains estimates of demand curves for household and sprinkling use for various areas in the United States, and even deals with peak-use demands as well as average daily demands. These relations have been used by any number of subsequent researchers and have not, to

69

Table 4.1

Water use in metered and flat-rate areas
(October 1963 through September 1965)

	Metered areas (10)	Flat-rate areas (8)
	(gal/day per dwelling unit)*	
Annual average		
Leakage and waste	25	36
Household	247	236
Sprinkling	186	420
Total	458	692
Maximum day	979	2354
Peak hour	2481	5170
	(Inches of water)	
Annual		
Sprinkling	12·2	38·7
Potential evapotrans-		
piration	29·7	25·7
Summer		
Sprinkling	7·4	27·3
Potential evapotrans-		
piration	11·7	15·1
Precipitation	0·15	4·18

* Gallons here and elsewhere in this paper are USA gallons.

my knowledge, been seriously challenged.

In Table 4.3., I first summarise the Howe-Linaweaver results for demand (and income) elasticities. There it is clear that sprinkling demands are generally quite elastic, but more so in the humid eastern United States than in the drier west where, I might add, the penchant for keeping green eastern-type lawns approaches fanaticism. But to get a more concrete idea of what this elasticity might mean to a water supplier, let us look at average daily demand per dwelling unit in an area having the mean characteristics of Howe and Linaweavers's twenty-one metered and public sew-

Table 4.2

Comparison of some estimated price and income elasticities
of demand for municipal water among some previous studies

Investigator	Year	Type of analysis	Price elasticity	Income elasticity*
Metcalf[11]	1926	29 Waterworks Systems Cross-sectional	−0·65	
Larson and Hudson Jr[12]	1951	15 Illinois Communities Cross-sectional		0·70
Hanson and Hudson Jr[13]	1956	8 Illinois Communities Cross-sectional		0·55
Seidel and Baumann[14]	1957	American Cities Cross-sectional	−0·12 to −1·0	
Fourt[15]	1958	34 American Cities Cross-sectional	−0·39	0·28
Renshaw[16]	1958	36 Water Service Systems Cross-sectional	−0·45	
Gottlieb[17]	1963	Kansas Cross-sectional	−0·66 to −1·24	0·28 to 0·58
Wong et. al.[18]	1963	North eastern Illinois Cross-sectional	−0·01 to −0·72	
Headley[19]	1963	S.F.–Oakland, 1950–59 Time-series		0·00 to 0·40
Gardner and Schick[20]	1964	43 Northern Utah Water Systems Cross-sectional	−0·77	
Bain et. al.[21]	1966	41 Californian Cities Cross-sectional	−1·099	
Turnovsky[22]	1969	19 Massachusetts Towns Cross-sectional	−0·05 to −0·40	
Wong[23]	1970	Chicago, 1951–1961 Time-series	−0·02 to −0·28	0·20 to 0·26
		Four Com. Sz. Grps. Cross-sectional	−0·26 to −0·82	0·48 to 1·03

* Income elasticity of demand is the ratio of the percentage change in demand to the percentage change in income. Its values are, with rare exceptions, positive, and the value 1·0 is used as the dividing line between 'luxuries' and 'necessities'.

ered cities, and let us see how this demand varies over a considerable range of prices. The results of such a calculation are shown in Table 4.4. Notice that doubling the price, from $·20 (£0·08) to $·40 (£0·16)/1000 gal. results in a 10 per cent decline in household use and a 53 per cent decline in summer sprinkling use. A further doubling of price induces a decline in household use to 69 per cent of its level at $·20/1000 gal.; sprinkling use is now only 21 per cent of its level at the original prices. In terms of total daily summer use, we achieve a 38 per cent decrease by the first doubling (to $·40/1000gal) and a further reduction of 24 per cent (of the original level) through the second doubling. Averaging this result over the year assuming that the sprinkling season is four months damps the effects. But even so, average daily demand per dwelling unit is reduced to 73 per cent of its original level when the price is raised to $·40/1000 gal. and to 51 per cent when the prices goes to $·80/1000 gal. Thus, the best available esti-

Table 4.3

Price and income elasticities for various demand
equations — from Howe and Linaweaver*

Areas	Quantity	Price elasticity	Income elasticity
Household use	Metered with public sewers (21)	−0·231	0·319
Summer sprinkling	Metered with public sewers (21)	−1·12	0·662
	Metered with public sewers − West (10)	−0·703	0·429
	Metered with public sewers − East (11)	−1·57	1·45
Maximum day sprinkling demand	Metered with public sewers (21)	−0·683	0·591
	Metered with public sewers − West (10) †	−0·388	0·438
	Metered with public sewers − East (11)	−1·25	0·931

* All results are for 'Equations of Best Fit' except for Maximum Day Sprinkling Demand − West, for which no price term appeared in the equation of best fit.

† Results corresponding to theoretical specification.

Table 4.4

Residential water use and its response to price based on the Howe–Linaweaver demand equations

I   Assumed characteristics:

   A.   Average value of dwelling unit: (v) \$20,800 (£8,320)

   B.   Average potential summer evapotranspiration *minus* effective rainfall (inches) $(W_s - 0.6r_s) = 10.91$[24]

II Howe–Linaweaver equations of best fit for 21 metered and public service areas:

   A.   Household use: $q_d = 206 + 3.47(v) - 1.30(p)$

   B.   Summer sprinkling use: $\log q_s = 1.09 + 2.17 \log (W_s - 0.6r_s) - 1.12 \log p + 0.662 \log v$

III Results:

p (\$/1000 gal)	Ave daily H.H. use dwelling unit	Ave daily summer sprinkling use (gal.)	Ave daily summer total use (gal.)	Ave daily annual total use (gal.)[25]
\$·20 (£·08)	252	467	719	408
\$·40 (£·16)	226	219	445	299
\$·80 (£·32)	174	100	274	207

mates of domestic water demand relations indicate that price increases can have very large effects indeed on quantities demanded by residential users.

On the industrial side, one would expect the situation to be at least this favourable to water pricing, simply on a priori grounds. That is, since one important determinant of demand elasticity is the availability of substitutes, and since plant managers presumably have available a wide variety of water saving technology, we would expect that industrial demands would be at least as elastic as that for residential use.[26] The evidence is patchier however, simply because data on industrial water use (and residuals discharge) have been held as company secrets. (In some cases, it appears that quantities of water use and residuals discharges are unknown even to management where plants are old, with water and sewer systems jury-rigged over decades.) But there are some indications available from industry studies done at Resources for the Future, and I shall summarise these briefly.[27]

In thermal electric plants, the significant use of water is for cooling the condensers.[28] Two questions are usefully distinguished: the design question, in which thermal efficiency and hence gross water use are variables; and the cooling tower (or pond) question, in which withdrawal only is variable. According to the supply and demand curves for thermal efficiency derived by Cootner and Löf, the choice of optimal thermal efficiency is very insensitive to cooling water costs. Indeed, it appears that the elasticity of gross water use (thermal efficiency) with respect to water cost is around -·01. On the other hand, the situation with respect to withdrawals can be depicted schematically as in Figure 4.1. At low withdrawal cost, condenser cooling water is used in once-through fashion. At some point, determined by local meteorological conditions, chemical costs, the opportunity cost of electricity and other factors, it becomes worthwhile to install cooling towers (or ponds) and cut withdrawals to 5 or 10 per cent of the once-through level.[29] Elasticity has almost no meaning on such a demand relation. It is, however, possible to give a rough estimate of the 'break-point' withdrawal cost, P_w. This value is given by the relation:

1   Choose cooling towers when: $\hat{P}_w \cdot W > \cdot 075W(\hat{P}_w) + (P_{ct})W$

where

W ≡ gross water use (1000 gal.),

P_{ct} ≡ average cost of cooling towers per 1000 gal.; and make-up withdrawals (to replace windage, evaporation and blowdown) are assumed to be 7·5 per cent of gross use.

We can rewrite the relation in 1 as

2   Choose cooling towers when: $\hat{P}_w > \dfrac{P_{ct}}{\cdot 925} = 1 \cdot 08 P_{ct}$

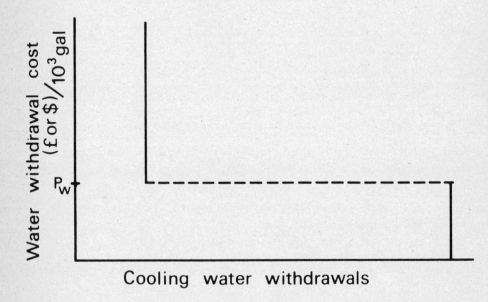

Fig. 4.1   Cooling water withdrawals in relation to water withdrawal cost

If P_{ct}=£·025 (£ 0·01), a reasonable figure for forced draft towers in the north eastern United States, the critical withdrawal cost is 2·7¢ (£0·011). In any event, it is quite straightforward to estimate for any particular region and even for a particular plant, what abstraction cost would be necessary to induce the adoption of recirculation. And cooling withdrawals are far and away the most important component of total industrial withdrawals.

The situation with process water withdrawals is far more complex since the options available depend, in general, on the nature of the process used, the product quality produced, other input qualities, etc., and hence the input water quality requirements and waste water residuals loads. [30] This implies that estimates of process water demand curves require fairly complete knowledge of the industry involved. In addition, because of the paucity of data, it is seldom possible to use multivariate regression techniques, and instead one must fall back on more or less systematic modelling at the process and plant level. Thus, Resources for the Future originally began working on a linear programming model of a petroleum refinery with water use and waterborne residuals included, in order to explore withdrawal (and waste water discharge) demand elasticities, and the impact of such exogenous factors as product mix and input quality. [31] Using this model we can explore the response of process water withdrawals to price, since the model includes a number of post treatment recirculation alternatives. [32] The results of a model run in which withdrawal costs were varied are presented in Figure 4.2. Notice that both desalter water cost and boiler feed-water costs were varied simultaneously, the former from $0·07 (£0·028) to $0·47 (£0·188) per 1000 gal. in steps of 0·05 (£0·02); the latter, from $0·15 (£0·06) to $0·95 (£0·38) per 1000 gal. in steps of $0·10 (£0·04). (These costs are assumed to include pretreatment.)

From Figure 4.2 it appears that considerable response to withdrawal cost is possible — total process withdrawals can be cut by over 80 per cent over the range of costs considered — but most of the 'action' is confined to a narrow band of costs from $0·22 / ·45 (£0·088/·18) per 1000 gal. to $0·32/·65 (£0·128/·26) per 1000 gal. The particular location of the band is sensitive to the estimates of treatment and recirculation costs used, but the narrowness of the response range depends on the characteristics of the process effluents themselves.

One cannot, of course, generalise to other industries from this result. In particular, the refinery study concentrated on recirculation alternatives for reducing withdrawals. For other industries, process changes may be possible and may become profitable over broader cost ranges. [33]

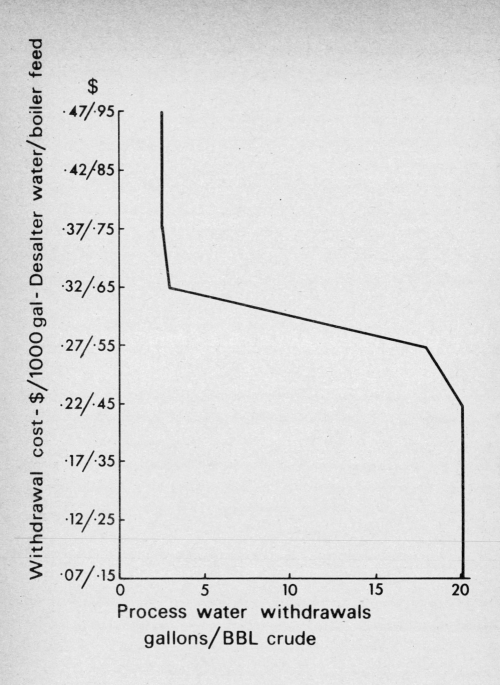

Fig. 4.2   The demand for process water withdrawals by a petroleum refinery

76

Pricing and the time path of water supply system capacity

It is natural to ask next what impact water pricing can have on the expansion path of a water supply system, for there is an argument that even if we observed an impact from metering and even if significant negative elasticities are estimated for demand functions, in fact these effects are temporary and disappear over time as people revert to old habits of water use. Under this argument an increase in price or the introduction of metering produces only a momentary jog in the curve tracing system use; after a few years total use will be exactly the same as it would have been in the absence of metering. [34]

In this area it would be useful to have retrospective studies of a large number of water systems in order to have enough information to separate the effect of price changes from other influences. Even one or two studies of systems which have consciously tried to influence their investment needs through pricing would be a start. So far as I know, however, no historical studies have yet been done, and we must fall back on simulation studies which are based on demand functions similar to those developed by Howe and Linaweaver. These studies are prospective and do not, of course, prove anything, but they do show what the best existing demand function estimates imply for system growth different price sets. I shall discuss two such studies in this section.

The first study [35] used Howe Linaweaver demand functions and generalised cost functions for capacity expansion [36] in a dynamic programming framework. The object was to find the capacity expansion and pricing policy combination which maximised net system benefits over some planning horizon. The study explored the sensitivity of a basic set of results to such factors as growth and discount (interest) rate assumptions, and different types of pricing structures, including increasing and decreasing block rates and a summer differential price.

The basic findings of this study may be summarised as follows: [37]

1 Increasing the price of water either delays or reduces the system capacity increments on the optimal expansion path. Hence, discounted future capital costs vary inversely with the unit price of water.
2 Under the particular assumptions made about cost and demand function parameters, the net system benefits were stable for prices from $0·10 (£0·04) to $0·40 (£0·16) per 1000 gal. Net benefits decline for prices above $0·40.
3 Results for increasing and decreasing block rates depend, for the all-residential system being studied, on the block rate ruling in the neighbour-

hood of 200+ gallons per day. The resulting optimal expansion paths are identical with those for constant prices at the levels of this block rate.
4   Summer rate differentials made no difference in expansion paths. [38] (This result is, however, an artifact of the particular kind of system simulated, and a closer look at distribution, as opposed to storage, capacity would probably change it.)

The second study of the dynamic effects of pricing which I wish to bring to your attention is that done by Boland, Hanke and Church for the Washington Surburban Sanitary Commission. [39] This work examined the impact on the path of demand expansion of a number of different pricing schemes, including regional and seasonal differentials. A chosen path of capacity expansion was taken as given and, in the aggregate, all pricing schemes had to produce enough revenue to cover charges and operating costs for the given system. Thus, the level of price was not really a variable of interest in this study.

In all, fourteen different pricing systems were examined. These consisted of combinations of the following elements:

1   Uniform Rates based on meeting all variable costs plus 86 per cent of annual capital cost of main facilities.
2   Separate seasonal rates with summer rates bearing the burden of capital charges.
3   Uniform Rates based on variable costs only.
4   Uniform Rates as in 1, but with services charges (per time period) reflecting sewer system costs as well as the residual 14 per cent of main water facilities capital charge.
5   Increasing block rate charges for residential customers.
6   Variation between the two main areas (counties) served by the utility according to a basically arbitrary allocation of system costs.
7   Variation over eight different service areas according to observed growth rate differentials.

The important results and recommendations of this study include: one promising policy was spatial variation in water rates based on observed growth rates. This would involve lower rates for the more densely settled and slower growing parts of the Commission area, and higher rates for the districts at the edge of suburban sprawl. The results were projected to be lower total water demands; lower sewer flows and lower sewer investment requirements. A significant potential drawback was seen in relatively high implementation costs.

An increasing block rate structure for residential use also appeared promising. This would effectively be a lawn sprinkling surcharge and would result in lower overall withdrawals and lower peak summer demands. (Recall the sensitivity of sprinkling demand to price in the Howe-Linaweaver demand functions.) [40] [41]

The other pricing systems considered were rejected for a variety of reasons. In some cases, such as seasonal pricing, it appears that the Boland et al. characterisations were not such as to give a fair test, so we certainly cannot assume that the final word has been spoken. On the other hand, it does seem that future investigators could safely abandon some of the more obviously faulty schemes, such as variable cost pricing where the long run social costs of encouraging larger demands and more rapid growth are ignored.

Pricing industrial residuals discharges

Although traditionally there has been great interest in the volume of industrial water withdrawals, the most important impact of industry on water resources is probably through residuals discharges. Except for some losses in cooling use and incorporation in products, industrial water withdrawals are returned to the water course. But when they are returned, they bring with them residuals from the processes in which they are used. Some of these residuals are simply solids or organics closely analogous to the residuals from domestic uses. Others, however, are 'exotics' such as heavy metals, complex petrochemicals, and chlorinated hydrocarbons, the effects of which on ecological systems are only dimly understood, though apparently potentially catastrophic.

Here again, there is a dearth of publicly available information. One can find any number of estimates of quantities of residuals from this or that type of plant. Indeed, there have been some attempts to identify residuals generation at the process level and to investigate the implications of changing process technology and increasing levels of treatment. [42] One cannot, however, find information on the potential response of industries to various prices on residuals discharge. In this situation, Resources for the Future has sponsored a number of industry studies (most of which I have referred to above) which in one way or another deal with residuals discharges. I shall briefly discuss a few of the results which have come and are coming out of these studies, but as a general preliminary observation, allow me to suggest that the lesson of all these studies is that industrial waste water discharges are potentially highly price elastic (where price is generally thought of in the form of an effluent charge per unit specific substance, such as ammonia, phenol, oil, etc.).[43]

The Löf-Kneese study of water use in the beet-sugar industry contains estimates of the costs of reducing discharges of BOD by various methods applied to the several process waste streams. These estimates are then combined to show the present value of the costs of achieving any level of discharge reduction for a typical plant.[44] From the total cost curves, a set of marginal cost curves are derived. Allowing for the fact that the marginal costs are stated in present-value terms, it is possible to predict the re-

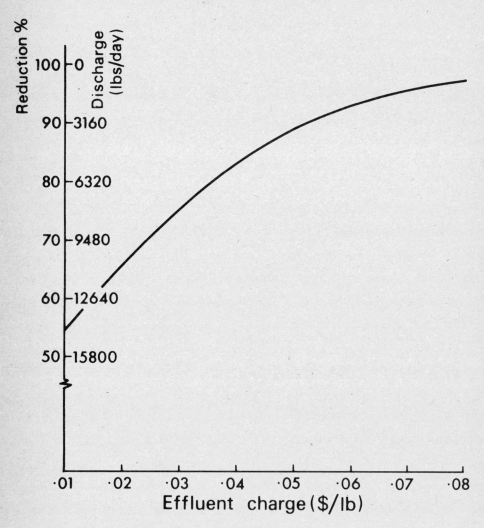

Fig. 4.3   Reduction in BOD discharges by a beet-sugar refinery (2,700 tons of beet processed per day) in response to an effluent charge

sponse of the sugar refineries to BOD effluent charges of various levels. Figure 4.3 traces the reductions in BOD discharges one would expect from a refiner having marginal costs characterised by Löf-Kneese's 'average rate, curve z' and facing effluent charges between $0·01 (£0·004) and $0·07 (£0·028)lb. of BOD. Because the Löf-Kneese marginal cost curve is smooth, the percentage reduction curve is also smooth and appears to become asymptotic to 100 per cent removal at charge levels above $0·08 (£0·032)/lb.

The petroleum refinery study deals with the response to effluent charges of a 150,000 bbl/day refinery. [45] The waterborne residuals considered are oil, BOD, phenols, ammonia and hydrogen sulphide and there is simply insufficient space to include here all the results obtained. But to give an indication Figures 4.4 and 4.5 are reproduced from the refinery manuscript. Figure 4.4 shows the percentage reductions in all five effluents in response to varying levels of an effluent charge on BOD alone. [46] Compared to the beet-sugar refinery, the petroleum refinery requires higher charge levels to produce similar removal percentages. Thus, the beet-sugar plant was predicted to go to 96·5 per cent BOD removal at a charge of only $0·07 (£0·028)/lb. The petroleum refinery achieves a 68 per cent removal in response to a $0·07/lb. charge, but only goes over 90 per cent removal when the charge is over $0·22 (£0·088)/lb.

Figure 4.5 represents, in a slightly different format, the response of the refinery to a charge on ammonia. [47] The interesting feature of these curves is the contrast between the 'basic' and 'advanced' refineries, which in turn arises from their quite different mix of processing units and hence of waste water streams. The basic refinery begins with a small ammonia discharge and reduces it by only about half in response to charges in the neighbourhood of $0.08 (£0.032) to $0.18 (£0.072)/lb. (of NH_3). The advanced refinery, on the other hand, has a rather large ammonia discharge at the zero charge level and reduces it by over 85 per cent in response to a charge of $0·08/lb. Analogous patterns hold for the BOD discharges which are also graphed in Figure 4.5.

As I have mentioned, other industrial studies are currently underway at Resources for the Future, including one of the pulp and paper industry and one of the integrated iron and steel industry. Furthermore, other institutions are also supporting work in this field. For example, the National Science Foundation programme in Research Applied to National Needs is funding a similar study at the University of Houston which concentrates on residuals management in various key parts of the chemical industry. [48] The Environmental Protection Agency is now soliciting bids for studies of a number of industries, but the time frame involved is so

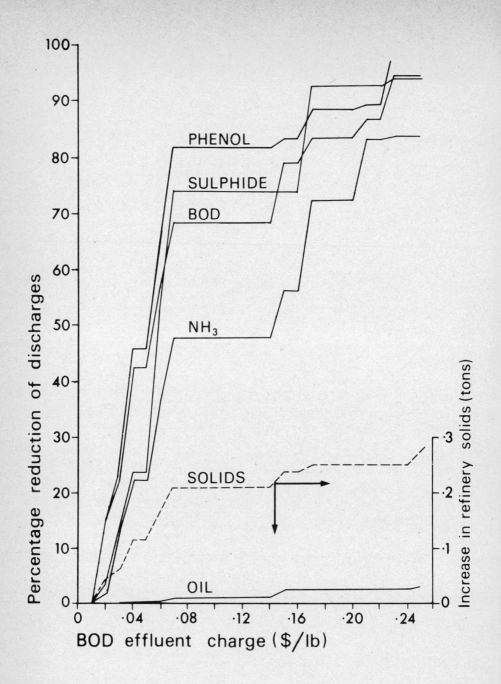

Fig. 4.4   Response to BOD effluent charge (basic refinery — benchmark product mix)

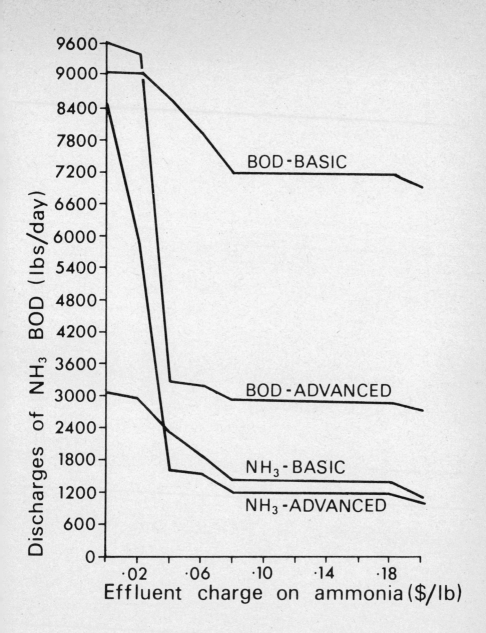

Fig. 4.5   Response to effluent charges on ammonia

short that one must be sceptical of the quality of the eventual product.[49] Nonetheless, it is encouraging to see interest in the industrial response to efforts to restrain the demand for the waste disposal service of the environment.

A final note: action in the real world

I have concentrated in this paper on a sampling of empirical evidence concerning the price elasticities of demand for water withdrawals and waste disposal services. But this is still one step removed from the reality with which many of the participants in this seminar have to deal. A final question is, then, whether men of the world are taking the arguments and evidence seriously and moving to institute such policies? I think the answer is yes, though my evidence is of necessity anecdotal. Accordingly, I propose to conclude by mentioning two interesting examples of current interest in pricing policies.

The state of Vermont, not generally noted as a spearhead of radical policies, has an effluent charge law on its books, though its enforcement is currently being postponed until next summer. Though the law is far from the economist's ideal, it could serve as a valuable example in the United States. Basically the law is designed to spur the completion of required secondary treatment plants by levying charges on dischargers not in compliance with the required treatment standard. The level of the charges is based on the prospective cost of secondary treatment to the discharger, with essentially arbitrary allocation to BOD, suspended solids and waste water volume, and with an adjustment for the size of the discharge relative to the receiving stream. Perhaps the most impressive testimonial to the potential effectiveness of pricing policy is the desperate opposition generated by this law when it became clear to dischargers just what was implied. The law was passed over a year ago, and the actual date of its enforcement remains anyone's guess.[50]

The state of Rhode Island has the smallest land area of any of the fifty states, and is quite densely populated. It shares with most of the north east, a tradition of strong and capable water supply utilities (generally publicly owned) which concentrate on 'clean upland sources' for their impoundments. Since Rhode Island is dominated by its capital city, Providence, the Providence water utility dominates water supply planning in the state. Using the requirements-projection technique, the planners came up with 'demand' figures which appeared to them to justify locking up 25 per cent of the total land area of the state in reservoir watersheds (traditionally closed to recreation in the north east). In addition, they ignored the impact these tremendous volumes of water would have when they were used and returned to the environment loaded with residuals.

Startled by the enormous implications of these proposals, an informal group of influential citizens, already formed as the 'Natural Resources Group', undertook to study the linked problems of water supply and waste water disposal in the light of Rhode Island's special geographical problems and of the existing national requirements for treating municipal and industrial waste water. The group's report to the governor and general assembly is an impressive document, and from the point of view of this seminar, its major recommendations are:[51]

1 ... it is possible and necessary through innovative planning to combine water supply and pollution control into a single administrative programme.
2 ... not only in future planning but in operation of existing systems, costs of pure water production and dirty water treatment should be linked. *The goal would be a fair assessment of the true costs on the user with improvement in conservation practices and, for the first time in the history of the state, effective pollution control.* (Emphasis in original.)
3 Expansion of the authority of the state Public Utilities Commission to set rates for sewage treatment costs, including combination of water/sewage where possible.

The NRG report is now the object of further study by a task force appointed by the governor. If the task force finds the recommendations to have merit, it is directed to write and introduce the necessary legislation to the state general assembly.

Thus, policies which are designed to restrain demand for water and waste water disposal through pricing are being taken seriously by some men of affairs on my side of the Atlantic. I recommend such policies for your consideration.

Notes

[1] In the sense used here, a price is a quantity of money charged *per unit of the good*. A charge per time period unrelated to water consumption (a flat rate) is not a price in this sense.

[2] Paul A. Samuelson, *Economics: An Introductory Analysis*, (7th ed.) McGraw-Hill, New York 1967, p. 60.

[3] The price elasticity of a demand curve at a point (or over a range), is defined as the ratio of the percentage change in quantity to the percentage change in price. Zero elasticity is roughly synonymous with 'requirement'. Since demand curves are nearly always downward sloping, price elasticities are nearly always negative. Common, if careless, usage involves speaking of absolute values without making this explicit.

[4] Since I am no longer working full time in this field I may have missed some valuable contributions.

[5] Charles W. Howe and F. P. Linaweaver Jr. 'The Impact of Price on Residential Water Demand and Its Relation to System Design and Price Structure', *Water Resources Research*, vol. 3, no. 1, 1967, pp. 13–32 (Table 1, p. 14).

[6] There is a large percentage difference in 'leakage and waste', but the absolute amounts involved are small, and Howe and Linaweaver do not discuss the statistical significance of this difference.

[7] *Modern Water Rates*, published by *American City Magazine*, 1965.

[8] 'Make Water Metering Universal', *American City Magazine*, vol. 69, no. 7, July 1954.

[9] Steve H. Hanke, 'Demand for Water Under Dynamic Conditions,' *Water Resources Research*, vol. 6, no. 5, October 1970, pp. 1253–61.

[10] This Table is taken from S. T. Wong, 'An Econometric Analysis of Urban Municpal Water Demand,' an unpublished paper from Simon Fraser University, Burnaby, British Columbia, p. 16.

[11] L. Metcalf, 'Effect of Water Rates and Growth in Population Upon Per Capita Consumption,' *Journal of the American Water Works Associa- (JAWWA)*, vol. 15, January 1926, pp. 1–22.

[12] B. O. Larson and H. E. Hudson Jr, 'Residential Water Use and Family Income', *JAWWA*, vol. 43, no. 8, August 1951, pp. 603–11.

[13] R. Hanson and H. E. Hudson Jr, 'Trends in Residential Water Use', *JAWWA*, vol. 48, November 1956, pp. 1347–58.

[14] H. F. Seidel and E.R. Baumann, 'A Statistical Analysis of Water Works Data for 1955, *JAWWA*, vol. 49, December 1957, p. 1541.

[15] L. Fourt, 'Forecasting the Urban Residential Demand for Water',

unpublished, University of Chicago, Department of Agricultural Economics, February 1958.

[16] E. F. Renshaw, 'The Demand for Municipal Water', unpublished, University of Chicago, Department of Agricultural Economics, June 1958.

[17] M. Gottlieb, 'Urban Domestic Demand for Water: A Kansas Case Study', *Land Economics*, 39, May 1963, 204–10.

[18] S. T. Wong, J. R. Sheaffer and H. R. Gotaas, 'Multivariate Statistical Analysis of Water Supplies', paper presented at the American Society of Civil Engineering, Water Research Engineering Conference, Wisconsin, May 1963.

[19] J. C. Headley, 'The Relation of Family Income and Use of Water for Residential Purposes in the San Francisco-Oakland Metropolitan Area', *Land Economics*, 39, 4, November 1963, 441–9.

[20] B. D, Gardner and S. H. Schick, *Factors Affecting Consumption of Urban Household Water in Northern Utah*, Agricultural Experiment Station Bulletin no. 449, Utah Sate University, Logan, November 1964.

[21] J. S. Bain, R. E. Caves and J. Margolis, *Northern California Water Industry*, Baltimore, Johns Hopkins University Press, 1966, chapter 5.

[22] S. J. Turnovsky, 'The Demand for Water: Some Empirical Evidence on Consumers' Response to a Commodity Uncertain in Supply', *Water Resources Research*, 5, 2, April 1969, 350–61.

[23] S. T. Wong, op. cit.

[24] Average effective summer rainfall for lawn watering is assumed to be 60 per cent of average total summer rainfall.

[25] Assuming a four month sprinkling season.

[26] Observed elasticities may be low because water costs are a small part of total costs, and thus do not receive much managerial attention.

[27] See also the results of Rees's large study of industrial water use in England, presented in Judith Rees, *Industrial Demand for Water: A Study of South East England*, LSE Research, Monograph 3, LSE London 1969. This study provides considerable evidence of the elasticity of industrial demand for purchased water.

[28] See the excellent discussion in P. H. Cootner and G. O. G Löf, *Water Demand for Steam Electric Generation*, Washington: Resources for the Future, Inc., 1965.

[29] Note that water consumption through evaporation will be nearly eqaul with and without cooling towers, since the same quantity of rejected heat must ultimately be transferred to the atmosphere whether from a tower or the stream surface. There will be some small difference because of cooling accomplished through 'bank cooling' in the stream.

[30] The many influences on industrial water demand were first systematically set out by Blair T. Bower. See, for example, B. T. Bower, 'The Economics of Industrial Water Utilization', in Kneese and Smith (eds), *Water Research* Baltimore, Johns Hopkins Press, 1966.

[31] This model has since been expanded to include airborne residuals and solid wastes. For the monograph describing it see C. S. Russell, *Residuals Management in Industry: A Case Study of Petroleum Refining*, Johns Hopkins Press for Resources for the Future, June 1973. A similar model for the integrated iron and steel industry is incorporated in W. J. Vaughan and C. S. Russell, 'A Residuals Management Model for the Integrated Iron and Steel Industry', a paper presented to a meeting of the American Iron and Steel Institute, Dekalb, Illinois, April 1973.

[32] Process water includes water used in the crude-oil desalting units and feed water for boilders making process steam, that is, steam that will *come in contact with* oil at some point.

[33] Such changes are discussed in another Resources for the Future industry study: G. O. G. Löf and A. V. Kneese, *The Economics of Water Utilization in the Beet Sugar Industry*, Washington, Resources for the Future, 1967. But unfortunately the information is not presented so as to make withdrawal demand curve construction possible.

[34] There is a technical argument which bears on this point. It is generally agreed that statical relations estimated on the basis of cross-sectional data reflect long run adjustments. Since most of the water demand relations have been estimated from such data, there is a strong presumption against the view that price changes lead to temporary reductions in use.

[35] Marshall Gysi, *The Long Run Effects of Water Pricing Policies,* Technical Rep. no. 25, Cornell University Water Resources and Marine Sciences Center, Ithaca, New York, March 1971.

[36] These cost functions were taken from Metcalf and Eddy, Engineers, *Comprehensive Water Supply for Orange County*, vols. I and II, New York State Department of Health, Albany, 1967.

[37] Gysi, *The Long Run Effects...*, pp. 174–75.

[38] That is, for a constant price of $\hat{p}$, and a summer rate differential giving $\hat{p}$ for the summer rate, the optimal expansion paths are the same.

[39] John J. Boland, S. H. Hanke, and R. L. Church, 'As Assessment of Rate-making Policy Alternatives for the Washington Suburban Sanitary Commission', Baltimore, September 1972.

[40] Hanke has been involved in research on water system pricing since about 1968 and has produced a number of studies in addition to the one discussed here. The reader interested in pursuing the subject further is referred to:

Steve H. Hanke and Robert K. Davis, 'Demand Management through Responsive Pricing'. *JAWWA*, vol. 63, no. 9, September 1971, pp. 555–60.

Steve H. Hanke and Robert K. Davis, 'Pricing and Efficiency in Water Resource Management', report to the National Water Commission, published by Natural Resources Policy Center, George Washington University, Washington, DC, December 1971.

Steve H. Hanke, 'Pricing Urban Water', *in Public Prices for Public Products*, Selma Mushkin (ed.). The Urban Institute, Washington, 1972.

[41] Charles Howe and William J. Vaughan produced a set of projects of aggregate urban demand curves for water in their report to the National Water Commission. These are not in the same category as the dynamic models considered above, but do reflect an extremely close look at projections of housing patterns over long time periods...See: Howe and Vaughan, Urban Water Demands, Appendix to RfF Report to National Water Commission, June 1970, available in xerox from RfF.

[42] For example, see *The Cost of Clean Water*, vol. III, Industrial Waste Profiles, US Department of the Interior, FWPCA, Washington GPO, 1967:

No. 1: Blast Furnace and steel Mills
No. 2: Motor Vehicles and Parts
No. 3: Paper Mills
No. 4: Textile Mill Products
No. 5: Petroleum Refining
No. 6: Canned & Frozen Fruits and Vegetables
No. 7: Leather, Tanning, and Finishing
No. 8: Meat Products
No. 9: Dairies
No.10: Plastic Materials and Resins

[43] In the case of BOD (biochemical oxygen demand), the charge is levied on the weight of oxygen which the organic residual will tie up in the process of oxidation.

[44] G. O. G. Löf and A. V. Kneese, *The Economics of Water...*, 102–3. These data have been corrected to 1968 dollars for Fig. 4.3 to allow comparison with other results.

[45] Clifford S. Russell, *Residuals Management in Industry: A Case Study of Petroleum Refining*, Johns Hopkins Press for RfF, June 1973, chapter 7 (1 barrel = 42 US gallons).

[46] The assumption is made in the study that the refinery is in the design

phase, so that the response to any particular charge level is a long run optimisation problem in which treatment plant capital costs are important.

[47] The words 'basic' and 'advanced' on the curves are shorthand descriptions of the product mixes and processing units for two different refineries. The 'basic' refinery is a standard US gasoline refinery. The 'advanced' refinery is making a product mix heavy on fuel oil, and including unleaded, low-octane gasoline. It includes modern hydrogen-intensive cracking processes.

[48] Professor Russell Thompson, principal investigator.

[49] Nine months is to be allowed for each study. The large studies at Resources for the Future each generally represent at least two years of work from inception to manuscript.

[50] For a rather complete discussion of the law see, Vermont Department of Water Resources for the Office of Research and Monitoring, EPA, *Development of a State Effluent Charge System*, February 1972 (16110 GNT 02/72). Those interested in even more detail could contact Mr John D. Hansen, Assistant Attorney General, who was the principal drafter of the legislation and implementation regulations.

[51] Natural Resources Group, 'An Integrated Program for Planning and Management of Water Supply and Sewage Disposal in Rhode Island', undated manuscript.

Discussion

Dr J. Rees: I want to bring the discussion back to Britain as I suspect that a number of you may feel that USA experience is irrelevant here due to the generally lower levels of both consumption and price. However, before doing this I must emphasis that the economists advocacy of unit charging is not for chargings sake, but to provide a useful tool for managing demands and judging consumer preferences. In the first place, pricing could be used to allocate water from existing supplies between different competing uses and users. Secondly, and clearly related to the first, price can be used to control water demands within available supply capacity. This control mechanism can be used at unusually low flow or peak demand periods, and at times when new capacity construction lags behind demand. The third major role attributed to the price mechanism by economists is as a means of determining which particular goods or services consumers would prefer to have produced in any one time period. Without a unit pricing system consumers are supplied with as much water as they like, irrespective of the costs and benefits involved, and they have no incentive to avoid waste or to save water. While the industry is probably justified in supplying all water needed to maintain health and hygiene standards, there would appear to be no rational reason for supplying water for waste or for 'luxury' use in gardens, dishwashers and air conditioning systems, unless people are prepared to pay the full costs involved.

The metering and unit charging principle has generally been accepted for manufacturing industry, and available evidence does suggest that manufacturers do respond to price rises by the introduction of such measures as recycling, slight product changes, and variation in the inputs used. However, strong opposition has been engendered by the suggestion that householders should also be metered. Basically, there have been four arguments against metering; the first that hygiene standards will deteriorate has largely been discredited today as there is no evidence of this occuring in other countries. A second common argument rests on the value judgement that water should be treated as a social service, freely supplied to all. However, any political decision made on these grounds should take place with clear knowledge of the costs involved. The third argument, that people are completely unresponsive to price is directly contradictory to the first, although it is not uncommon for both to occur in the same article; for example, in the emotional anti-metering piece written by Christopher Price in the *New Statesman*. This view, and the fourth argument that the costs of metering will exceed the benefits, are open to verification or refutation by empirical testing.

At present the only area where such testing is possible in Britain is Malvern, although data should become available shortly from a metering experiment in Fylde. From research done in Malvern it appears that there is a very significant difference between household consumption there, where the price in 1959 was 20p per thousand gallons, and consumption elsewhere in Britain where the effective unit price was zero. On average consumers in Malvern take 24 per cent less water than they do elsewhere, and the only convincing reason for this is that householders have responded to a metering situation. Not only that, but from study of the effect of price changes on the time-trend of household consumption, it would appear that an increase in price of 10 per cent would reduce water usage approximately 1−2 per cent in most types of property. The price elasticities calculated for Malvern were very close to those found by Howe and Linaweaver for internal use in the United States. However, there was little evidence to suggest that consumers here were more highly responsive to price during the summer months.

Although responsiveness to price changes is relatively small, it appears large enough to allow the viable introduction of metering in some high demand, high supply cost areas in England and Wales. Certainly, I believe strongly that great savings would accrue from metering a new town like Milton Keynes, or the projected settlements around Maplin. However, we cannot know with any degree of certainty whether unit pricing will have the desired effects unless more metering experiments are conducted. I will end with a plea that more of you follow Fylde's example and begin controlled experiments in different areas and amongst consumers with different socio-economic characteristics. Not only will these improve our knowledge on the effect of pricing but they should also help us in the development of econometric demand forecasting models.

Mr D. Wilkes: Economic measures are not the only means of restraining demand. Curtailment can be achieved either by voluntary appeals, by planning conditions, or by the use of penalties.

Appeals for a voluntary reduction in consumption can be made when the immediate supplies are adequate but reserves are not fully replenishable. This can arise when the long term demand on an aquifer or reservoir exceeds the natural recharge. During drought periods voluntary curtailment of water use for essential household functions has also proved to be successful. Appeals of this nature are often useful as a first measure when attempts are being made to conserve supplies. They may also be used whenever an authority is unclear about its powers to take other measures. In this situation, however, care must be taken to ensure that the appeal is either applied equally to every user or is applied on the basis of priorities which have previously been assigned to each user.

The second type of curtailment arises in the planning process. In Britain local authorities have the power to enforce certain standards with respect to water supplies before giving discretionary approval. This is a five stage process and at each it is possible to reject the application on the grounds of inadequate water supplies. During the first three stages, approval of town plans, outline approval, and structural approval, the Department of the Environment, and through it the River Authorities and water suppliers have a chance to comment on the plans. Whilst during the two remaining stages, withdrawal consent, and consent to change or increase in use, it is the responsibility of the new Regional Water Authorities to make representations to the planning authorities.

Finally penalties have often been used as a last resort to obtain a reduction in consumption. Penalties would be invoked for excessive use, disobeying by-laws or disobeying directives and these would be enforceable by law. Some countries, however, have often relied more on regulatory rather than penal powers and these involve the cancellation of licences for excessive use of water. In both cases it is probably the knowledge that civil penalties have been, or can be used, which is most useful in bringing about a reduction of consumption.

Mr B. Rydz: I want to make a few comments on Dr Russell's paper. I would quarrel only with its title, 'Restraining Demand', which I think is loaded. We must distinguish between measures designed to get a true economic response and words like 'restraint' with their puritan overtones. We must do this because restraint over and above any explicit economic limitation (externalities and all) has a fashionable following. Perhaps in the fullness of time these people will even be proved right.

In this country I think the problem falls into three areas. The most important is the one that Dr Russell dwelt on most, and that is the direct supply of water to industry out of rivers and the receipt of effluents back into the rivers. Here we have a charging system in each River Authority area. Dr Rees criticised it, but I think it is a fairly sensitive system and one designed upon the right lines. I entirely agree with Dr Russell's suggestion that we should develop a complementary system of effluent charging. There has been a good deal of resistance to this. Many people have said that it cannot be done because it would be too complicated. I believe that it can and must be done, and I think we have to operate this in conjunction with ambient standards for reaches of the river. Our beloved Royal Commission standard started life as a means of preserving ambient standards. It is our folly that has degraded it into a discharge standard. I think that Germany and the Netherlands are moving in the direction of ambient standards although the USA and Canada seem to be retreating towards discharge standards at the moment.

The second area is the supply of water to industry by water undertakings. Normally this is on meter and is sold at about the price it costs to produce. We are doing here more or less what the economists would demand of us. The weak link in the chain here — and I believe this is true in charging for supplies out of rivers too — is that more often than not the industrialist has not the information at his command to make the right response. I do not think we should deceive ourselves about this. Most industrialists do not have enough knowledge of the costs which any particular level of water use imposes throughout their factory; they may not be in a position to separate the water handling in their internal costs from others. Therefore, we are not likely to get easily the right response to any changes in water price.

The third area, which Dr Rees touched on particularly, is the domestic area. The dominating consideration there is that we do not have metering in this country, and we can only talk realistically of getting a response to water costs if we are willing to contemplate domestic metering. I think that Dr Rees touched on most of the relevant issues there. I think there is fairly wide agreement that there is some elasticity, but there is a lot of disagreement as to whether the response will be worthwhile or whether you will have any positive saving at all after paying for metering. I was looking very recently at a paper produced by one of my economist colleagues in which he tried to assess for this country the future water costs at which the introduction of meters would be justified; my impression is that we are well short of the point at which one can justify the universal installation of metering. In the dearer water areas we are somewhere near that point. I would like to echo what Dr Rees said about having a few more experiments in selected areas. On the other hand, let us recognise that there is an immense built-in political resistance to the introduction of metering. Considering that economically it is such a debatable move, and bearing in mind the strength of this resistance, we probably have rather more important things to consider at this stage.

Mr D. J. Kinnersley: I connect garden sprinkling very much with the use of lawn fertiliser. If people have spent £5 or £10 on fertiliser, they will not have it wasted. I would therefore ask the fertiliser firms what the growth of lawn fertiliser sales is. This is a subject on which the water industry might well keep its eye, as well as on the sale of sprinklers.

I am very much in agreement with Dr Russell's remarks on the case for effluent charges resting on the continuing incentive. I think it is unfortunate that Professor Beckerman has tended to argue about the perfection and the economic efficiency of the virtues of pricing as against regulation. I think that that argument is not as convincing for reasons that have come out rather well in the incentive argument that Dr Russell put. I welcome his laying stress on that.

On effluent charges, I wonder what the effect of the volume charges is. I have heard it suggested that because effluent charges have risen in Birmingham, there has seemed to be a marked decline in the rate of increase of water consumption, suggesting that industrialist may not be very price-sensitive when they take water but do become sensitive if they find the stuff is expensive to get rid of. Therefore a charging system that put a premium on volume disposal as well as a premium on the disposal of difficult effluent might have quite a bearing on water demands simply because industrialists react to the cost of getting rid of it more than to the cost of taking it.

Lord Zuckerman: I associated myself with Professor Beckerman in the report entirely because charges implied an incentive. I cannot imagine an adequate regulative scheme which is not based on more information than is available at the present moment. Sooner or later it will be necessary for the authorities to know what is going into the sewers or rivers. Once that happens, charges should constitute an incentive.

Sir Norman Rowntree: Arising from the remarks or Dr Rees and Mr Kinnersley, I endorse the need for much study in this subject. It is a very difficult subject to study, and given that it is difficult, it requires a lot of hard work. I would like to be sure that the experiment is well designed, not in the conext of what we are doing now but of what we are almost certainly going to be doing in the future. I would like to see experiments in the future based on a combined charging scheme for water supply and effluent disposal.

Sir Frederick Warner: On the point about why industrialists are more sensitive to charges on effluent, this is a question of price. The Drainage of Trade Premises Act, 1937, makes it compulsory for the local authority to receive industrial wastes as required by an industrialist. The authority can levy a charge for the reception of that waste. So we have in the majority of cities of this country a system which amounts to what Sir Norman is asking for as a combined charge. Industrialists pay on the meter for fresh water, and pay for discharge and treatment on the volume of the discharge. This is charged for in three ways on the volume − one way on the actual volume related to the capacity of the sewers, one way on the cost of pumping and the third on the cost of treatment. There is also a charge for the disposal of suspended solids. We have many effluents being charged for by local authorities at 60p per thousand imperial gallons, whereas the fresh water costs only 20p.

I was worried about the proposal for placing charges for effluents put straight into watercourses. In this case you do not have the same method of pricing because you do not have a method for determining the charges for purification, but can only work by standards which are related to the capacity of the system, and these are not standards in terms of analysis but of mass balances. In practice where there are industries along the estuarial Thames, these are regulated by sharing out the capacity of the river and requiring the industrialist to accept a standard corresponding with how much of this capacity he is going to be allowed. This is possible because the power to do this is given to the Port of London Authority under their Act, and not to any other River Authority.

Mr D. J. Kinnersley: The argument that you can charge for disposal to sewers because you are charging for a service has one small fault which is that the charge at the sewage works depends on the sewage works effluent to the river. If you doubled the standard of effluent to the river you would have to increase the treatment charge. There is therefore an element of using the river in a sewer charge.

Lord Zuckerman: Sir Frederick used the term 'mass balance'. If you are going to partition the possible load of pollutant in an estuary, you could partition much more if less overall was going in.

Sir Frederich Warner: You have to allow also for the increase in industry; but one of the things brought out particularly by the third report of the Royal Commission is that in effect the advances made in the reduction of pollution are due to technological advance and not to other mechanisms.

Lord Zuckerman: The technological advance might be spurred by the financial incentive. It is time we got more up to date information.

Mr J. McLoughlin: On the proposed effluent charges, there is a big distinction to be made in regard to charging a man who is discharging into sewers, because once the agreement is made he has a right to discharge into the sewers. With rivers it is different because the riparian owner downstream is entitled to that water with no sensible alteration in character. If you impose these effluent charges, are you then going to give the man a right to discharge into the river, or is he still to be liable to have to pay compensation or submit to an injunction from someone downstream who goes to court and wants him stopped altogether?

Mr B. Rydz: I think those common law rights would have to be converted into a claim against a river management authority – a demand that it set a standard.

Mr J. E. Beddoe: We have made a positive proposal in that field already.

Mr P. L. Ashford: Where a river and catchment have surplus resources both to supply water and absorb effluent, the present system encourages the wasteful use of these. It is in many cases cheaper for an industrialist to take twice as much water as he really wants merely to dilute his effluent. He can be fairly sure whether he takes 100,000 or 200,000 gallons a day that he will get a 20/30 standard imposed on him. If he has the higher quantity of water, he is able to dispose of twice the pollution load into the water. He only pays for an abstraction, and if he has a private abstraction, in many River Authority areas the cost per thousand gallons for this is extremely low. So unless you introduce a charge also on the effluent discharge, based not on the volume but on the total pollution load you do not encourage the proper use of resources at present.

Mr M. Nixon: Surely the River Authority has a remedy. It can alter the terms of the licence. This is the real control on the amount abstracted from the river.

Mr J. M. Boon: I would like to defend the public water supply undertakers. One of these days a water charge will be based on every usage of water. All my working life I have been engaged in the supplying of pure and wholesome water, where the quantity that is wanted by people to be delivered to the house is delivered, and very cheaply indeed. I meter my own personal supply and know exactly what happens in my house, and it works out approximately as the department wants — that is, that the charge that we make in my area per thousand gallons almost exactly equals the charge a normal household pays by way of rateable value — 10p per £ of the rateable value, which equals 20p per thousand gallons of water. That is jolly cheap. The increase by a percentage is very difficult. If you put 10 per cent on the water charge, they think you are breaking their necks; in point of fact, 10 per cent of next to nothing is next to nothing — and I say that in the presence of scientists. They would probably argue against that; but I am certain that water charges for domestic supplies should enable the people to take as much as they want for their domestic use and that the charge is still low. It could be doubled and trebled, and it would make no significant difference to the general public of the country. The poorest classes who cannot afford 20p to 30p a week could be subsidised in the way that they are subsidised now.

I hope that when the water charges are merged with the sewage charges the effect will not be too bad. I believe very strongly indeed that, whatever the cost, by the year 2000 we will have to meet, and should meet, a doubling of the demand, and I believe the public will be willing to pay that amount for it, because it is cheap and necessary. Any idea of curtailment is to my mind retrograde.

With regard to industry, I think my company was the first company in the country which introduced a maximum demand scheme for industry. We decided that before we would supply large food processing factories, which took two to three million gallons a day, they would have to give us in advance an idea of their take. We assessed them on the capital we had to spend to bring them that water, and we assessed a maximum demand charge on a daily basis. If they exceeded it for over three days they came into a higher figure.

I say again — water is jolly cheap; you could double and treble the cost and it would still be cheap. I hope you will take the view that we ought to get it whatever the cost and not go in for restricting it in any way.

Mr G. W. Curtis: On the question of cheapness, there is a point which the economists ought to look at. As I understand the Ministry's intention with the RWAs, sewerage is going to be self-supporting financially just as water is. If one has a general rate covering sewerage and water, the cost is going to be fantastically high in rural areas, when one remembers that the cost of sewerage in some areas is as much as £1000 a house. If the grant structure disappears from this and it has to become self-supporting and linked with water, you will have to put the water costs up twenty times.

Mr J. E. Beddoe: No, you are not right. The rural areas will benefit because of equalisation.

Mr G. W. Curtis: Sewerage is more expensive than water.

Mr J. E. Beddoe: In the past people have tended to talk about pollution charges and charges for water in two separate compartments. You only get sense in this field when you look at the whole system.

Mr D. A. D. Reeve: Comments made about the Birmingham scheme are largely accurate. A substantial proportion of the cost to traders is in respect of the volume they take up on sewers and in treatment works and in respect of treatment the volume charge currently represents 46·7 per cent of the total cost. There is difficulty in a trader sometimes installing means of measuring the quantity of the effluent he is discharging and my authority is prepared, as a means of overcoming this difficulty, to use as a basis for the charge, the supply of town water which is variably metered, with an adjustment made for that proportion which is used domestically on his premises. The proposal draws to the attention of the manufacturer not only the charges that will arise due to the treatment of industrial effluents, but also the cost to him of taking town water. In several instances, this awareness has resulted in a reduced consumption of potable water with the consequent reduction in trade effluent discharge.

Mr R. J. Bell: Dr Rees gave us four reasons against metering domestic supplies. Might I add a fifth one for consideration? It is this. There are 6000 consumers in my authority's area who take water through a meter, and they have this water by agreement. The fact that domestic supplies are not under this form of agreement makes it possible for an authority — although nobody likes to do this — to put restrictions on the supply, particularly in the case of the use of water for garden purposes, during times of severe drought.

5 Multiple Use of Water

B. R. THORPE

> One may not doubt that, somehow, good
> Shall come of water and of mud;
> And, sure, the reverent eye must see
> A purpose in liquidity.

Rupert Brooke

Recreation, Sport and amenity within the water cycle

The Department of the Environment in its publication *Background to Water Re-organisation* suggests that six million people in Britain regularly engage in inland water-based leisure activities, a figure which does not include ramblers, campers, bird watchers and other casual users of water space. If we accept this figure then American experience suggests that we ought also to accept that where there is now one visitor to water resources — in ten years time there will be two and in twenty years, three. Why? — Because water has an irresistible appeal to people the world over and nowhere more so than in Britain with our island heritage and seafaring traditions. Increased and better training in the enjoyment of outdoor activities will cause people to seek even more often the regenerating power of nature on the human spirit.

This is the Minister's Fourth Dimension and success in this field may do more for the proposed new Regional Water Authorities than any other single feature of their activities. The public have grown used to a wholesome and unlimited supply of water — equally there will be no medals for providing an adequate sewerage service — it follows that many may judge the new Authorities by the improvements they can make to amenity and by the extension and widening of recreational opportunities. Progress in this sphere will have a direct effect on the richness of life and it may be useful to look for a moment at the clauses in the new Bill which are designed to provide the framework within which the new Authorities can pursue these objectives. Under clause 19 each water authority is to be under a statutory duty to make the best use of the water under its control for recreation and amenity with what we hope are adequate powers for this to be done. It will be necessary to carry out a comprehensive review of available water space in order to see how it can best be developed for sport, recreation, conservation and amenity. The Bill also preserves those provisions in the Water Resources Act, 1963, relating to the preservation of amenity and public rights of access, as well as the provisions in the Countryside Act regarding the desirability of conserving the natural beauty of the countryside. To soliloquise on the long term opportunities which the Bill provides is tempting, but may I turn instead to discuss a number of points where the process of re-thinking may lead to a radical change in attitudes and practice within the next few years.

River engineers working within the provisions of the Land Drainage Act, 1930, have considered flood relief, improved farm drainage and clearance of rivers as a primary duty. Efficiency in conducting these operations has steadily improved over the years. Nevertheless, even though food production is still of major importance, engineering principles and economic viability must be exposed to a new philosophy of life. We must ask, is this scheme, this practice, really acceptable when you add the Fourth Dimension? Civil engineers are not Philistines, but they have been asked to carry out tasks where amenity has rarely been raised as a top priority. A straightened river, a drained swamp and an embanked channel meant drainage efficiency — not vandalism — just a missing parameter in the equation for carrying out works. The river must be considered as part of a basin in which the whole cycle of water use is surveyed and that Fourth Dimension involving people is given prominence.

A value will be put on the intangible — the potential to give pleasure. The river may meander round clumps of trees and over brickbuilt weirs complete with fish ladders, providing a setting for the angler to relax in peace watching his float in the gin clear runnels between the weed. An ideal state! Maybe, but this is what we could aim at and this is where change is already taking place.

Each Regional Water Authority must have suitably qualified staff capable of taking advantage of amenity and recreational opportunities and of putting into practice policies laid down by the new Water Space Amenities Commission. They must be consulted at the planning and preliminary design stage of all works and be prepared to advise on landscaping, ecology and the requirements for leisure activities within the region. They must work closely with the County Councils in providing access to rivers, lakes and reservoirs and fostering a wide variety of water based leisure activities. Advantage must be taken of the assistance and advice which water recreation interests on the Regional Sports Councils can give, and consultation with amenity, conservation and sporting interests will be time consuming, but necessary. In no other area of the Regional Water Authorities will there be more opportunity for local involvement. American practice in the water world is not always ahead of our own, but they have developed a rapport with the public which is worthy of adoption here.

The Institution of Water Engineers' Report *Recreation on Reservoirs and Rivers*, published in 1972, comments favourably on the results of experience in the use of reservoirs by the public over a number of years, and in paragraph 4.1 records: 'Where in the last decade access to the water's edge has been permitted, there is no evidence to show that significant direct pollution has resulted.' Sailing, angling and bird watching are all possible on the same reservoir with proper planning and management. It will be an obligation on the new Regional Water Authorities to promote water based activities through liaison with the local authorities. Access to the water's edge both of reservoirs and rivers will require a high priority.

There is no evidence from recent experience on inland waters that a wide variety of leisure pursuits are incompatible in themselves and further that they give rise to significant pollution problems. Provided of course, and this point is stressed in the recent IWE report, that effective management, control and supervision are instituted. There are reservations about bathing and water skiing on direct supply reservoirs, but sailing clubs operating on, say, afternoons only are perfectly compatible with angling, which might well thrive on a morning and late evening time schedule.

The key to recreation on or near water is the provision of social centres and car parking so that the public can be accommodated in large numbers without giving rise to the random contamination of the countryside by litter and dumped waste.

It seems to me that capital outlay on landscaping, even in the style of Capability Brown in the eighteenth century, with its emphasis on tree planting and contouring, can be a worthwhile investment. Perhaps one need not go so far as to provide ha-has and herds of deer, but at least new reservoirs should be joyful places! The indented shoreline and the tree draped curve of a river can give that element of surprise and delight which is at the roots of our enjoyment.

Water undertakers have found that fishing and sailing activities can be made to pay for themselves and with the provision of a social centre a whole range of other activities such as picnicking, bird watching, rock climbing and nature study can be followed without seriously affecting the primary function of the water space which, in most cases, is to provide treatable water of good quality at reasonable cost. Mr Hookway, director of the Countryside Commission, in his paper to the Association of River Authorities Conference 1972, 'The Pleasures of Water', proposed a new creed for water conservationists: 'It is my duty to ensure that people can enjoy the necessities and the pleasures of water.'

May I also quote Count Leon Lippens's introduction to the International Union for the Conservation of Nature's publication *Liquid Assets*:

> The protection of Nature was a concept unthinkable to our forebears of a hundred years ago. Nature was hostile, the traditional enemy of man. One had to clear forests, reclaim marshes, cultivate, 'put to good use', take possession of small parts of the earth's surface ... so man set out to conquer ... and then he realised that the earth is neither unlimited nor inexhaustible ...

I have already mentioned the subject of river engineering and the change in attitude that is coming about. With the call not only to preserve but to enhance the natural setting of our rivers and lakes, the conservationist must consider the origins of the water which supplies streams and lakes – taking a good look at vegetation, the soil structure and the area's geology. In America, for example, marshland has sometimes been reclaimed by drainage only to leave deserts or at best thin crops barely justifying the effort put into the altered use. And in train of this activity, that vital commodity water is squandered in winter flushes followed by droughts in summer. Streams become flashy and the soil structure is destroyed – rare plants are lost and the birds depart to other ever decreasing habitats.

It is being said repeatedly by present-day experts working in the field of world health and the environment, that only land with a good potential for arable farming should be drained by pumping or other expensive means. We in Sussex have a raised bog in one very low-lying area – inaccessible but of great scientific interest. The whole area is capable of being drained by pumping. Here is a ready-made problem for the young Regional Water Authority. To preserve the dragonfly, the snipe and the kingcup in the wild brooks, or tame the area to corn, crop spraying and midges. If we were operating under American law we should be called upon to prepare an Environmental Impact Statement of quite incredible length – we need not over react but the basic thought processes ought to be the same.

Three million anglers are reported to fish on our rivers, lakes and in the sea at some time during the year. The next most popular water sport is boating – 700,000 participants. Ian Drummond in his paper to the Association of River Authorities' Congress on 'The Future of our Rivers' gives figures of 209,000 acres of inland water existing at present in this country (including 55,000 acres in lakes and reservoirs). To meet water resource demands another 40,000 acres of new reservoirs may be provided by the year 2000. How many miles of the 20,000 miles of inland rivers and how many of those 55,000 acres of lakes and reservoirs are accessible to the general public? Not the largest proportion by any means, and a proportion of what remains is unacceptable because of the levels of pollution. Indeed a large proportion of the three million anglers live in the industrial areas where pollution is worst. It is in these areas that lagoons in flood plains and on the washlands of river flood relief works could be used as fish farms and hatcheries. The growth rate of fish on shallow flooded grass is very high as has been demonstrated by catches in early years on Chew Lake and other new reservoirs. Our water space resources are modest and we must seek to make the best use of all of them.

Streams and rivers have a natural power of regeneration and it is only economic good sense to use this capacity for self-purification in our cycle of water use. The Royal Commission standard laid down at the turn of the century (twenty BOD, thirty suspended solids) related to an eight times dilution to the effluent in the receiving stream. The receiving watercourse in Weald clay areas rarely gives more than a two to one dilution in summer, and perhaps a mile of stream has to be considered as a further process to the normal treatment. This fact must be recognised, and provided the effluent is consistently up to 20/30 standard the end product is often acceptable. With a number of works discharging to the same stream a continuing process of regeneration would be anticipated from outfall provided that the discharges were far enough apart. A problem we must now face is the linking of several districts under a joint sewerage scheme where a large new works is situated further down a river system, thus bypassing several miles of channel with recuperative potential. It may be that new sewage disposal works could in some instances be situated at the upper extremity of sewerage areas so that a degree of recycling of water is carried out. This would mean that river intakes would be below effluent discharge outfalls and the onus on the new Regional Water Authorities would be to treat the waste to a standard where the regenerative powers of the natural river would assist the purfication process so that abstraction to public supply would not cause undue problems in treatment processes.

Apart from the sixty million plastic containers floating around in the Pacific Ocean and the millions in other seas which turn up on remote Antarctic shores, we are also slowly polluting our seas with toxic matter resistant to degradation. Sea birds are laying sterile or soft shelled eggs in the Shetlands because their food chain is contaminated in the Gulf Stream by effluents emanating from the USA seaboard. Thus we must seriously consider the extent to which we are misusing the capacity of the sea to purify. Ought we to stop further discharges of untreated waste to the sea? It is basically a matter of cost − are we prepared to pay more for an improved environment or must the quality of life diminish gradually for the lack of caring?

Oil, sewage and plastic debris on the wrack line of our beaches diminish the enjoyment of the shore and we often add to this desecration by sea defence works of compelling ugliness. It is little known that River Authorities have sea defence responsibilities along a substantial proportion of our coastline, and large areas of lowland have to be protected by shingle banks and dunes. But as the coast is increasingly protected against erosion by groynes, sea walls and embankments, so we often destroy the appearance of our beaches. Sea walls themselves become a source of difficulty often involving the further loss of natural beach. If we wish to make our beaches more attractive and pleasurable to the public then we might find the answer in imitating nature − the shingle and sand is our natural defence against the sea, and rather than man-made structure as a defence we could replenish the beaches with naturally graded sand and shingle dredged from deposits in deep water offshore. In Kent, recharge is an established sea defence process on the Pett frontage and in Sussex a gleam of hope is now appearing that the Selsey-Bracklesham front will receive a substantial boost of marine ballast dredged offshore.

Recharge, recycling, regeneration, the three 'Rs' of the 1970s − these are the processes which the new Regional Water Authorities will develop and in doing so care must be taken to ensure that the Fourth Dimension is included as an important factor in each one of them.

Discussion

Lord Zuckerman: I do not know whether Mr Thorpe wishes to discuss the paper and the general theme which emerges from it, or to arrange for some local travel agency to take us either to Sussex or to those parts of America to which he referred.

What opportunities have we in this country for such grand amenity schemes and what would we be prepared to surrender in order to bring them about?

Mr M. Nixon: Mr Thorpe was kind enough to say in his paper that engineers are not Philistines, and he then proceeded to explain that we always behave like them! However, I must congratulate him on delivering a paper on multiple use without ever using the phrase, and I want to bring you back to multiple use.

What we have seen is just one facet of river basin management. The engineers have cause, and all of us have cause, to quantify the amount of water required to provide for all sorts of facilities, and it is in this area that we do find difficulty in reaching some reasonable forecast of the quantity of water required for the enjoyment of the public in the recreational fields.

The first point I want to make is, how do you define a river? I always like to define a river in terms of its flow regime. A river's function is two-fold: it is for the disposal of surplus surface water and for the disposal of waste. In the natural river the waste is the natural detritus from erosion, in a river in an urban setting its physical ability dispose of waste is used for the disposal of man-made waste. This factor should be optimised, and therefore one should not abstract or use the water of the rivers so that this physical ability to dispose of wastes, both fluid and solid, is in any way prejudiced. The 1963 Water Resources Act said that the way we ought to do this was by defining what was described in the Act as the minimum acceptable flow, and that was a flow which was sacrosanct; in other words, you should not permit abstraction below this level of flow so that the river could meet all its requirements and behave like a river. If you over-abstract from a river, then, because it is a self-adjusting system, it will readjust to the new climate of flow. Thus it will silt and reduce its width and thereby impair its ability to transmit the relatively unmodified peak flows.

To give you some idea of the amount which is currently used in my area, I give the figures for the mean daily abstraction from the River Trent − these being figures of use of water in terms of percentage of mean daily flow of the catchment area. The amount abstracted for public water supply is 22·3 per cent, industrial use is 6 per cent, cooling is 135 per cent, milling is 40 per cent, and agriculture is 0·36 per cent. It may seem odd that the demand for irrigation water should have been the one which really triggered off the need for the 1963 Act. This arose because the demand was completely uncontrolled and seasonal. Therefore actual abstraction during the growing season is significantly greater than the figure given. The fact that these figures add up to more than 100 per cent is merely an indication of the amount of re-use in the river system.

In order to preserve the quality of the river the total amount abstracted should not exceed the minimum acceptance flow. I think that this figure is the amount which Mr Thorpe needs for his recreational use so that the river is not a sort of muddy ditch; it has to have enough water to support fish, to allow sailing to look pretty, and so on. I think that this could be about 40 per cent of the mean daily flow. Earlier Mr Rydz showed that natural storage during drought conditions produces on average about twenty million cubic metres per day. As the average daily value is 190 million cubic metres this shows that natural storage under drought conditions would provide about 10 per cent of the mean daily flow. Therefore, it would appear as though natural storage does not provide a sufficient residual flow in the rivers during drought periods to meet the demands for abstraction and recreational use.

Dr R. D. Hey: I would like to comment on one of the points Mr Nixon has raised. He suggested that any abstraction below the minimum acceptable flow would result in a readjustment of the channel to a new climate of flow. I think that this is unlikely to be the case because rivers in this country are adjusting their shape and dimensions to the flow which, in the long term, collectively transports most material. Calculations have shown that this dominant flow has a return period of .1·5 years on the annual flood series which, in turn, is the return period of bankfull discharge.

Consequently abstraction of water below the minimum acceptable flow will have no effect on the capacity of the channel in the long term because the river is in adjustment with the relatively unmodified intermediate flood discharges. Abstraction below this value will only really influence the chemical and biological quality of the river and not its physical dimensions.

Lord Zuckerman: You now have some numbers applied to your pictures, Mr Thorpe, and I wonder whether you would care to comment on their significance.

Mr B. R. Thorpe: May I first answer your original point about the applicability of American practice to English conditions? We do have areas of grandeur, the Lake District and Wales, for example, where we could improve our facilities, but generally speaking the ability to reach our water is confined to smaller numbers of people. What I do say is that we could take from the Americans some of those ancilliary facilities which were so apparent as a part of the main feature — the barbecues, the covered camping sites, and so on, facilities which we just do not have on the scale and of the quality that the Americans have. I think we could look at some of those facilities and try to apply them to our landscape, even though we do not have the grandeur or the abundance which the Americans enjoy.

Lord Zuckerman: Since you have provided a part-answer to my question, may I ask another? Is there any absolute limitation to what could be done in the small settings of this country? You referred to barbecues, but every barbecue also has a parking area. I understand from friends in the Peak District that the authorities there are already overloaded by motor cars, and that the major danger to amenity areas in our small country is that before you know where you are, the trade which you stimulate turns beauty spots into barbecues.

Mr B. R. Thorpe: The Peak District has one answer in that it has kept the motor car out of certain districts and people have to make a bigger effort to get there.

Lord Zuckerman: If you were a planner, would you say that you could organise one of these areas where you could have a barbecue and a picnic area but not an area into which you could bring your car and offload your boat?

Mr B. R. Thorpe: We are bound to recognise our limitations. I think there are areas like that.

Mr S. V. Ellis: I have been very disappointed with the new Bill. After hearing the Minister speak about the Fourth Dimension, I thought that the Bill would provide something wonderful. Some of us were saying before we saw the Bill that it had got to provide money. All that the Bill says is that it shall be the duty of every water authority to take such steps as are reasonably practicable for putting rights to the use of water and any land associated with the use of water to the best use for the purposes of recreation. To start with, we do not know what our rights to water are. We have a slight extension of the 1963 Act which said that subject to this and that, a river authority may, if it appears reasonable, permit the use by members of the public for the purpose of recreation. The new Bill has gone a tiny step forward by imposing a duty instead of a permissive power.

I am very disappointed that this Bill has not found us some money for recreation. Another Clause of the Bill says that each function has to pay for itself.

My Authority joined in a study on the multiple use of water on the Broads. When we had got out all our wonderful plans, we considered where the money was to come from. First, there were the boats that use the Broads. An exercise was done as to how much money would be required to carry out our grandiose schemes, and it was obvious that it could not come from the boats. The tolls would have put them out of business. We have not found the answer yet. We have done a big exercise and have come to a full-stop on the question of cash.

I would like to know how much better off we are under the Bill with this Fourth Dimension.

Mr J. E. Beddoe: The money comes out of all of us. You are big enough to find the money. You are big enough to carry the cost yourself now.

Mr S. V. Ellis: The function has to carry its own costs. Recreation has to find its own money. How do we do it?

Mr R. C. Chilver: I cannot quite see why, if the people who want to use the Broads for boating do not want it badly enough to pay what it costs, people who do not go there should pay the difference. I regard it as rather unfortunate if this Bill repeals the provision in the Water Resources Act that taking one year with another, the recreational function must pay for itself.

Dr C. Russell: I want to second what Mr Thorpe said. I think that the problem with the places in America is that they do not charge anything for their use. This is traditional with most of our water based recreations. It seems to me that if you provide the recreation free, you will get the problem of excess use. You have got to make people pay for recreation. Getting the money and keeping the quality are the same problem. Of course you run into the problem of people saying that this is not socially equitable and that they should be provided with these opportunities. This is what is behind the American experience. We are unwilling to redistribute income as income, and so we redistribute services. Thus we have the free use of services by people who could afford to pay for them.

Mr D. J. Kinnersley: Unless you charge very large amounts of money, you cannot get enough revenue to finance the recreational amenity. So, like Mr Ellis, you say you cannot do it because you have not got the money. Mr Ellis then says that he does not wish to be associated with the kind of rich patron that RWA No. 5 would be, taking its money from the towns and spending it on the Norfolk Broads; he wishes to be segregated to Norfolk. He then faces the dilemma that either the Norfolk people must finance it and keep it to themselves, or it must be financed by people outside Norfolk who, if they pay for it through one route or another, are going to feel that they have some right to turn up and park their car against the Broads they helped to pay for.

Mr S. V. Ellis: If it could be paid for out of the revenues of large regional authorities ...

Mr D. J. Kinnersley: I think you and I understand the Act differently.

Mr J. E. Beddoe: The Act says that it must balance its accounts as a totality, not each segment of them.

Lord Zuckerman: What would be wrong with charging ten times as much as you now charge for having a boat on the Broads?

Mr S. V. Ellis: This was the argument that I was using this week in a small working party, that the licence fee is a negligible proportion of the cost of running a boat, getting it here, and maintaining it. In fact they could bear a much larger charge.

Lord Zuckerman: On this argument, would amenities not be improved if a lot of people were deterred from coming too easily?

Mr S. V. Ellis: Do you cater for the public or for one rich patron? Where do you draw the line in such a case? Do we let the public come, or

108

do we price them out of enjoying the amenities?

Sir Norman Rowntree: It is not the cost of the licence which puts people off, but the cost of the boat.

Professor K. M. Clayton: The fee that I am charged for keeping a boat on the river is 2 per cent of my annual cost. This seems to me to be quite ridiculous. The hire boat industry has simply persuaded the local River Authority that it would be quite untenable to increase the toll. I think it should be tested.

Mr D. Ruxton: When looking at the Dee estuary scheme the county councils were involved, and they felt that they should have an interest in the finance and control of the recreational part; they also felt that while there should be clubs which paid high fees there should be a separate area, which they managed which would be for direct public access. Both sets of facilities were needed in their view. Whether this would work out in practice I cannot say.

Lord Zuckerman: What we have here is a good illustration of the interface between political and social questions on the one hand, and changing use on the other. Who is going to resolve the problem? Will it be resolved by those who feel that the Broads should be cultivated to whatever extent people wish without putting up licence fees, or should one discourage people from coming? So far as the Bill is concerned, we have been told that it is the total accounts of the RWA that matter, and not any particular part of those accounts. We could start with Mr Thorpe's descriptions of multiple use in America, to see what the potential demand is; over here we see what happens when one starts changing the actual use of the river. Then we get to the political considerations.

Mr D. J. Kinnersley: From my own experience in managing water recreation, there is the commercial consideration that if you start putting the charges up, which we desperately needed to do and did at quite a rapid rate, you do have to accept much more of a contractual commitment to provide something that appears to be worth the higher fee, and this in turn raises your costs considerably. There is the problem that managing recreation is labour-intensive in various ways, and the person who pays the higher costs will want the locksman not merely till 6 p.m. but till 8 p.m. or 10 p.m. on Sunday night. One reason why the authorities do not charge commercial rates along the Tyne is that they prefer to treat the user as a person who is getting a very good bargain and they know to that extent that they are not completely committed to providing the sort of services that an expensive golf club does. If you compare the expensive golf club with municipal golf club, you have a comparison.

Lord Zuckerman: Consider the present public dispute about charges for museums. When free, the museums were as well served with curators as anyone could wish. Here was a free public service. But the protests when asked to pay a nominal charge. I speak with some knowledge here because one of my responsibilities is to look after a public institution which has always charged – the Zoological Society of London. We know the problem. But equally we know that we cannot put up our charges just as we would like or reduce the quality of the services we provide. When I talk about the quality of the services provided, I am thinking about the visual impact, the animals, and the public.

I return to Dr Russell's point, that the American problem has been created because no charges are levied. I think I am right in saying that at certain times of the year people now avoid the Grand Canyon because the crowds who go there are said to destroy its grandeur. That seems to be the major problem with all amenities – if they work, and the public is encouraged to go, they become over-used. They decline in 'quality', and you then have to start again somewhere else. I come back to the simple point that I made at the beginning – if we do provide a barbecue, can't we exclude the motor car?

Mr J. McLoughlin: In the main these facilities will be provided at the discretion of the RWA. The only duty to be imposed on them will be to take such steps as are reasonable for putting their rights to the use of water and of any land associated with water to the best use for purposes of recreation. But their rights to the use of water or such land will be limited, and not normally extend to rivers.

In exercising this discretion they will face a conflict of interests. Each RWA will be a major discharger of sewage effluent, and the conflict will be between use of the river for this purpose, and the promotion of recreational facilities and protection of amenity. In the first place there will have to be consent conditions for sewage effluents, and it is not yet clear how these will be determined. Secondly, compliance with the conditions will have to be secured. The odd result of this legislation will be that the RWAs themselves will have duty of enforcement.

The question arises as to who is to ensure that the RWA complies with consent conditions in discharging its sewage effluent. Under the Rivers Prevention of Pollution Acts the power to prosecute for offences under the Acts is limited to River Authorities and other persons with the consent of the Attorney-General. In practice the power has been exercised entirely by River Authorities, who have in each case used their discretion whether or not to prosecute. This power will be transferred to the RWAs, and there is no indication that the limitation will be removed. Obviously the RWA will not be able to prosecute itself, and one can expect private prosecutions with the consent of the Attorney-General only as exceptions. Clearly therefore, the conflict of interest which we have noted will be resolved by a decision within the authority, and, subject to outside pressures, we can expect the RWA to resolve it in its own favour.

In the absence of any legal compulsion, some degree of public accountability is needed, otherwise members of the public will have no means of influencing the authority if they are dissatisfied with the standard of recreational facility or amenity which is maintained.

At present there is a statutory majority of local authority representatives on River Authorities. These people are nominated by local councils. Members who are nominated by a representative body, and thus one further step removed from the electorate, in practice cease to be accountable to that electorate. Despite this statutory majority, therefore, the River Authorities are not accountable to the public of their areas. Similarly the new Regional Water Authorities will not be accountable to the public.

In these circumstances there is good reason for removing the restriction on the power to prosecute, and reverting to the Common Law position. At Common Law any person can bring a private prosecution if he so wishes. If this restriction were removed, members of the public, perhaps backed by interested angling or conservation societies, could take steps to ensure that once standards for discharges are established they are in fact enforced. Otherwise the RWAs will remain safely insulated and be able to relax standards virtually at their discretion.

Such a change would confer a further advantage on individual members of the public. Under the Criminal Justice, 1972, Section 1, when a court, including a magistrate's court, convicts any person of a criminal offence it can award a compensation order of up to £400 in favour of any person who has suffered loss, damage or injury as a result of that offence. This can be a simpler and cheaper way of obtaining compensation, providing a criminal prosecution can be launched.

Mr D. J. Kinnersley: Mr McLoughlin said that the conflict would be resolved in the Regional Water Authority's favour. He then went on to treat the Regional Water Authority purely as an effluent discharger, whereas the real significance of Clause 19 is that it has a duty to see that all the water it has rights over is suitable for amenity, and therefore the term 'resolved in its own favour' is so to speak meaningless unless you recognise that it has its duties. It has the duty to get rid of effluent and it has the duty to promote amenity. It is that conflict which has to be resolved. The words 'in its own favour' do not really answer it at all.

Mr J. McLoughlin: The RWAs will have no duty to promote amenity. It will have a duty to take such steps as are reasonably practicable to promote recreational uses where it has rights to the use of water. What are these rights to the use of water?

Mr J. E. Beddoe: They vary enormously. They may own the whole of the fishing rights and navigation. They may have nothing but control of the discharge of effluents.

Mr J. McLoughlin: If they own a reservoir, they own it completely. With the rivers, they do not own the river itself. Therefore, apart from their rights of abstraction, there are no rights there to which Clause 19 applies.

Mr B. Rydz: Is not the answer to establish target conditions for these river reaches of the sort that we were discussing earlier by the same process of public consent as attaches to minimum acceptable flows under the 1963 Act? Surely one could seek a process under which these target conditions for reaches of rivers have to be established in the face of the public, with a procedure for appeal, and thereafter have statutory force? It is then a matter of whether the Regional Water Authority is working through its consent conditions towards the standards that have been imposed upon it by statutory process. I should have thought this was the kind of guarantee by which members of the public could be protected.

Mr S. V. Ellis: We had this in the 1951 Act. A River Board could make by-laws for different parts of the river. The provision was dropped because it would not work.

Mr J. E. Beddoe: The reason 'reasonably practicable' is there is that if you have a reservoir for public water supply, that use must have primacy.

Mr J. McLoughlin: I do not object to those words.

Mr J. E. Beddoe: The River Authority has a complex of duties. It inherits a duty to maintain and improve the quality of the rivers.

Mr J. McLoughlin: Once a consent has been given, why cannot a member of the public take steps to ensure that it is enforced?

Mr M. Baldwin: I should like to turn attention to another legal aspect of multiple water use. Take the case of a canoeist prosecuted for disturbing anglers' rights to fishing. How can you reconcile the two along a stretch of river when such a legal tangle exists?

Mr J. E. Beddoe: There are many people who want to use the limited amounts of water available. Inevitably there will be conflicts; you cannot do everything. On a big reservoir you can sometimes separate sailing, bird watching and fishing. But there cannot be compatibility of all uses at the same time.

Mr D. J. Kinnersley: The private ownership of water is a problem of very long standing in this country, and the short answer to the point about canoes is that the River Authorities, the Country Landowners' Association, the National Farmers' Union and the British Canoe Union are trying, with limited success in certain parts of the country, to get access agreements for canoeists to use water to which they have no legal right of access, but the problem is, of course, that in a stretch which the canoeist wants to use there are very many riparian owners, whereas an angler could be satisfied by making a deal with one riparian owner. The traditional private ownership of fishing rights in this country does make the organisation of canoeing a particularly difficult thing to do. We are doing our best and making rather slow progress but it is not for want of trying.

Mr J. McLoughlin: That is a very sound argument for having some degree of representation of sporting organisations on the RWA so that their interests can be looked after. With the Regional Sports Councils in being, this would be very easy indeed.

Lord Zuckerman: I should hate to be the representative!

Professor P. O. Wolf: I should like to comment on some of the points that were brought up earlier. Mr Thorpe raised in the gentlest and most attractive manner the very difficult problem of conflict between various uses. Then Mr Nixon spoke of the flood aspect. I think we should not forget that the disposal of surplus surface water − I am quoting Mr Nixon − at unusually high rates completely interferes with a number of other uses, particularly amenity. The question in some cases of ensuring that amenities can be enjoyed safely is something that needs to be mentioned, although in view of the shortness of time we probably cannot discuss it.

Mr M. Nixon: What we have been talking about for the last fifteen minutes is the whole concept of river basin management, and we are going to do it for the benefit of the majority of the people. This inevitably means some form of rationing because we just have not got enough facilities and enough water to go round. In fact, on the Trent we already ration the water space by restricting water skiers to certain lengths of the river because they are incompatible with fishing, but this can be done amicably and it is part of the system of management. This is what the Bill is all about.

Mr B. R. Thorpe: The Basic truth that the discussion has illustrated is that people's requirements for amenity and recreation are as varied as the people requiring them. I doubt if we shall ever reach the stage where people will know the name of their Regional Water Authority representative, but I would say that this is an area of activity where I think the Regional Water Authorities have a special duty to get close to the people they are serving. The Americans have got their style of facilities because that is what the Americans require. They have taken the trouble to seek public involvement and find out what people want. I think that we ought to follow the same procedures here so that the public decides whether it wants exclusive facilities at high cost or more generally available facilities at low cost. I think the message is public involvement, and this is the area of activity in which the Regional Water Authorities must be most conscientious if they are to secure general acceptance.

Lord Zuckerman: I fully agree. Public involvement in the USA with the kind of problems generated by the use of wilderness areas is different from what we call public involvement here, which at present consists mainly in conflicting propaganda by minority groups. The canoeist wants to curb the angler and the angler wants to stop people disturbing the fish. In the USA you get university groups sitting down with the people concerned with amenities.

Dr C. Russell: I think there is monumental confusion about what happens in the USA; I wish the situation were that happy. In fact, I believe that river basin management by a quasi-executive body, which is somehow supposed to absorb the 'will of the people', is a discredited notion in the USA.

We both certainly face the same problems, but if you hold my country as an example, you are mistaken. On the other hand, I believe you have to find a better way than that provided by the Bill to get public involvement in amenity decisions. We both have two systems: the market and democratic representation, and we have not yet used either of them effectively to make decisions in this area.

Lord Zuckerman: When you have found out how to correct the mistakes perhaps you may be in time for the Act which will follow the particular Bill we are now considering!

6 Management of Water in the Coastal Zone

Professor A. VOLKER

Introduction and problem identification

One might wonder why in a seminar on the management of water supplies special attention should be paid to the conditions in the coastal zone. Typical water management problems of today, like rapidly growing water demands, limited water supplies, environmental changes and others, are essentially the same in the coastal as in the inland zones. In this paper stress will be laid on problems specific to the coastal zone rather than on the general problems of water management.

There are indeed some special features which distinguish the coastal zone. Differences are found not only in the physiographic setting but also in economic and human factors.

Man has always been attracted by the sea and Great Britain is perhaps a prime example of this bond. Besides the psychological factors, there are, of course, several material economic factors which explain man's preference for settling in the coastal zone. Looking at the world as a whole approximately one-third of its population is living in low-lying areas with an altitude of less than 200 m above mean sea level and within 100 km of the coast. No less than 650 million people are living within 50 km of the sea. There is certainly a concentration of population, agriculture and industry in the coastal zone, and it is here also that the world's largest cities such as Tokyo, New York, London and Rotterdam are found.

A substantial part of this coastal zone, often the most productive and densely populated, consists of the lower reaches of river valleys, low-lying coastal areas and deltas. Indeed the earliest civilisations like the Egyptian, Mesopotamian and Indian cultures, developed in these areas because they present a number of natural advantages such as fertile soils, abundance of water, easy communications, flat topography, etc. These advantages however are partly offset by inherent drawbacks and certain problems have to be overcome in order to get the full benefits of such areas.

Special problems in the development of coastal areas are:

1   Defence against the tides and especially against storm surges. Abnor-

mally high sea levels, sometimes several metres above the high levels of the astronomical tides, are known to occur on many coasts like those of the North Sea, the Gulf of Bengal, the Gulf of Mexico, the west coast of the Pacific Ocean and others. Perhaps the greatest disaster of this century was the cyclone on the Gulf of Bengal on 12 November 1970, causing hundreds of thousands of casualties. For the first time in history reliable data on sea levels were obtained indicating a level of 6·3 m (21 ft) above mean sea level at the delta front, with a wind effect of around 5 m.

2 Drainage of low-lying coastal lands. Land at an elevation of several metres below mean sea level is not only found in the Netherlands, but also in Denmark, Egypt (the polders in the delta of the Nile near Alexandria) and Japan. It represents the efforts and financial sacrifices of people in the densely populated coastal zone in order to increase the arable land area.

3 Maintenance of harbour entrances. In almost all navigation channels in deltas permanent dredging is necessary to maintain the required depths. This forms a heavy burden for such ports as Rotterdam, Rangoon, Bangkok, Saigon, Nagaya and many others.

4 Salt water intrusion. This is the most important problem of water management in coastal zones. It is dealt with in the next paragraph.

Water management problems of a more general character, like water, soil and air pollution, and environmental problems caused by changes in land use, are perhaps more pronounced in the coastal zone than elsewhere. This is a result of the higher concentration of population, the greater vulnerability of the ecosystem in the transitional zone between the fresh and the saline water, and the repercussions of human intervention in the rapidly changing channel system in deltas and estuaries.

There is a close relationship in low-lying coastal areas between the interests of water management, defence against the tides, drainage and navigation. Deepening of navigation channels for instance promotes the intrusion of sea water which endangers the water supply. Land drainage promotes the subsidence of the land making the defence system more vulnerable and also promoting salt water intrusion. An integrated approach is necessary considering all interests jointly.

At the same time the coastal zone forms part of the adjacent river basins, and in keeping with the concept of integrated river basin development, it would be rational to plan the development of the water resources of the higher and the lower portions of the river basin as a joint development. History shows however that the development of deltas — like those of the Nile, Rhine and Mekong — has not waited until upstream development in the field of flood control and water conservation by reservoirs, erosion control and pollution abatement had taken place.

The conclusion must be that whereas in the coastal zone there is a problem of reconciling the interests of water management with other interests, there is also the problem of reconciling the interests of this zone with those of the upstream portions of river basins. This may be particularly difficult in the case of international rivers.

Hydrological problems in the coastal zone

As mentioned already the main problem is that of the intrusion of saline water. One can distinguish various 'sources' of salt. There is some salt contained in the rain fall of the coastal zone, and also salt particles in spray carried by the wind. However the amounts are small compared with those from other sources.

Navigation locks are important as entries of sea water. During the opening of the outer gates the lock chamber is filled over its entire depth with sea water from outside. With the opening of the inner gates this water can spread into the fresh water canal. The entrance of sea water at navigation locks was recognised as early as 1667 by a Dutch scientist named Henri Stevin. Recently methods have been developed to reduce such salt penetration. A simple and inexpensive means is a pneumatic barrier whereby air bubbles are injected across the entrance to the lock. Eddies generated by the rising bubbles help to prevent the interchange of saline and fresh waters. A more drastic reduction is obtained by removing the saline water admitted to the lock chamber by pumping this water back to the sea and replacing it with fresh water.

A third source of salt is produced by seepage of brackish water from aquifers into the subsoil. This water comes to the surface in areas below the level of the surrounding land or water. The aquifers may contain water of high salinity due to marine transgressions during geological history. The seepage water may be drained off as a saline effluent, contaminating the recipient surface waters.

Another supply of salt to the coastal zone is the salt load of the river. This salt may originate from certain geological formations in the river basin, or it may be supplied as drainage effluent from saline soils, or as a waste product from industries. Thus the saline contamination of river water is often very pronounced in arid zones or in industrialised areas. The river Rhine, for instance, at present carries some 340 kilogrammes of chlorine at the German-Dutch border causing an average salinity of some 150 and a maximum salinity of more than 400 ppm of chlorine.

The fifth source of salt is formed by the intrusion of sea water into open estuaries. This source is the most difficult to analyse and to control. By virtue of its higher density the sea water intrudes over the river bed in an upstream direction mixing with the fresh water above it. Such saline contamination can extend inland some tens or even some hundreds of kilometres from the mouth. Deepening of navigation channels in the river causes the intrusion to extend still further as exemplified by the case of the entrance channel to the port of Rotterdam, where a clear controversy exists between the interests of port development and the interests of water management and quality control.

Water abstraction upstream (for irrigation and filling of reservoirs) diminishes the riverflow and also causes an increase in the saline intrusion. The intrusion can be halted by increasing the upland discharge. This can be achieved by diversion or by release of water from reservoirs. To obtain a significant effect a substantial increase in the flow is required which implies an uneconomic use of fresh water.

Water conservation in the coastal zone

The considerable demand for water in the coastal zone caused by concentrations of population and industry are still further increased by the requirements of salinity control. The salt water intrusion can only be partly checked and to maintain an acceptable quality of surface water a flushing or rinsing of open water courses, such as irrigation or drainage canals, is necessary. This again requires high amounts of fresh water. Thus in the overall water balance of the Netherlands about 40 per cent of the total water need is required for flushing the canals. This figure does include the minimum flow which needs to be maintained in the open estuaries.

To supply sufficient water during dry periods, storage during periods with water excess is essential. This storage can be found in upstream reservoirs, but the problem of storage allocation and rational reservoir operation which then arises is particularly delicate in the case of international rivers. Hence storage possibilities must primarily be sought inside the coastal zone.

When previously man settled in deltas and low-lying coastal zones he found water in the pockets or lenses of fresh water beneath dunes, former beach ridges and natural levees along rivers, where rain water had accumulated. This form of storage is still used; the water is of good quality but the yield is small compared with modern needs even when artificial recharge by river water is applied. Man also built tanks, or more or less

118

watertight reservoirs, in coastal lands to store fresh water drained off during the wet season. This ancient system is now being revived in the Netherlands primarily for the storage of water destined as drinking water. The reservoirs are filled during periods in which the river water is of acceptable quality.

Desalinisation of sea water is perhaps the most recently introduced source of water supply in coastal areas. It is not only used in arid zones where fresh water is very valuable, but also in such a relatively 'wet' country as the Netherlands. The distillation plant at Terneuzen (Dutch Flanders) yields some 28,000 m³ of fresh water per day. By this means fresh water can be made available, but only in comparatively small amounts and at relatively high cost.

To create really substantial storage capacity and to control adequately the water resources, the physical framework must be drastically changed. This is achieved by enclosure of estuaries, tidal embayments, gulfs and lagoons. The original saline water is removed by sluicing or pumping, and fresh water can then be stored in such reservoirs. The enclosing dam shortens the coastline, thus providing a new line of defence against storm surges and reducing sea water intrusion. Schemes of this type are multi-purpose, and can also serve to improve the drainage of low-lying land and facilitate communications by water or land. A part of the enclosed area can also be reclaimed and used for various purposes.

With land becoming more and more scarce, water demands increasing, and upstream storage potentialities being already used, the creation of coastal reservoirs by damming off tidal inlets has become very attractive. This is shown by the large number of successful schemes of this type in Japan and the Netherlands, two countries where the effects of land scarcity and water shortage are strongly felt. In both countries recent storm surges (1959 and 1953 respectively) demonstrated the inadequacy of the coastal defence system. In Japan the works of Kojima Bay and Hachiro Gata are cases of enclosure and partial reclamation of an embayment or lagoon. The works on Tone River (near Tokyo) and Nikko River (near Nagoya) are estuary enclosures. In the Netherlands the enclosure and partial reclamation of the Zuider Zee (1932) is a classical example of the first type. It was followed by the enclosure of the Lauwerszee, the Braakman, the Brielse Maas, and after the disaster of 1953 the damming off of the estuaries of the Rhine and the Meuse. Similar schemes are now being studied in England, and also in Korea, Bangladesh, Cuba, Singapore and India. Mention should also be made of the recently implemented scheme at Plover Cove, in Hong Kong, although this one differs in some respects from those mentioned above.

When examining the technical and economic feasibility of coastal reservoirs some specific features should be duly considered. Compared with upstream reservoirs in mountainous areas, coastal reservoirs have a relatively small variation in water level, and evaporation losses play an important role in the water balance. The outflow depends on the tidal levels and there may be periods when evacuation is hampered. Still more critical is the salt balance. Coastal reservoirs are also exposed to salt water intrusion, and to keep the salinity within acceptable limits some drainage towards the sea is necessary. This point may be decisive in the feasibility of such schemes especially in arid zones. Underground inflow of brackish ground water, as in the Braakman in the Netherlands, may prevent the reservoir water from becoming sufficiently fresh. An accurate prediction of salt balance is therefore absolutely necessary and may require special investigation. Special attention should also be paid to the prevention of leakage of sea water at sluice gates, and the reduction of salt admitted by the locking of ships.

In most cases the economic feasibility depends largely on the costs of the enclosing dam, and especially on the costs of the final closing operation. With a large tidal range, a considerable acreage to the tidal basin, and moveable sandy or muddy beds along the line of the dam, closing the last gap is a major operation requiring special techniques such as bottom protection, use of closed or open caissons acting as temporary sluices, cable ways, etc.

There are certainly drawbacks attached to this type of storage, and in some cases it may be economically more attractive to store water in tanks built on the tidal flats in estuaries rather than transform the entire estuary into a freshwater basin. But this, of course, provides a much smaller storage potential.

As in all fields of hydraulic engineering, water management of the coastal zone, and transformation of the natural environment, is a matter for careful weighing of pros and cons and studying alternatives. The fascinating aspect which has always attracted man lies in the development of the meeting place of land and sea.

Discussion

Lord Zuckerman: I should like to express my gratitude to Professor Volker for being with us today. We are immensely grateful to him because the experience which he can bring to bear in this seminar is of considerable interest. Mr Eldon Griffiths yesterday indicated how much our future

120

arrangements will have to be concerted with those of Europe in general now that we are members of the same Community.

Professor P. O. Wolf: Professor Volker and I have known each other for twenty years, and I have always felt that the international courses at Delft were particularly fortunate in having a practising engineer and scientist of his stature as a visitor. In a little over half an hour he has given what I imagine would be a six months course at Delft and raised so many absolutely vital points that we shall be embarrassed by the complexity and number of them.

Professor Volker has listed a number of important factors, and I wonder if it would be possible for him to say which are in fact the dominant ones. Is it a problem of scientific knowledge? Yesterday Sir Norman Rowntree said he felt that the scientific facts were pretty well established, and it was the political and economic picture which was much more difficult to tackle: does Professor Volker agree?

Another question in scientific terms, again related to the national economy, is one of priorities. Is it in fact navigation which, nationally or internationally, presents the greatest danger to water management, or is it the difficulty of reconciling upstream to downstream requirements? Professor Volker used the word 'controversy' rather than 'conflict'. I believe there is a straight conflict. I am not trying here to be a mediator but trying to establish whether Professor Volker feels that if one gives advantage to one side it would be at the expense purely of the other side. I am hoping that Professor Volker can give us a clear indication of what it is that we should first concentrate on.

Lord Zuckerman: Is Professor Wolf's question related to coastal management in this country or to coastal management in general? Each country appears to have different priorities and different purposes. Are our problems today the same as when the Fens were established? Are we also experiencing the salting up of coastal lands as is Holland? I would like to know whether the priorities are general or particular to different countries.

Professor A. Volker: Professor Wolf has raised a difficult question. It depends very much on the particular conditions of the country and the area. Professor Wolf asked which of the factors I consider to be the significant one. Is it in the political field, the economic field, or the environmental field? That question is closely related to the next point about priorities.

I will start first with the psychological effect — at least in my country — and then I will try to extrapolate a little. There is one psychological factor, and it is that experience is not transferable from one generation to

121

another, or only to a very limited extent. It is the case now, and it has always been the case, that a new generation is never ready to accept the experience of former generations. Each generation has to learn its own lesson with regard to the battle with the sea. The sea is very treacherous: it may attack you today and it may not do so for another 200 years, and then it may come back again two weeks later. Thus the generation which has witnessed disaster is more inclined to accept the solution. the drastic solution, the counter-offensive — that is, the enclosure of an estuary. That is clearly seen in the Netherlands where all these schemes were initiated immediately after a disaster. Then some twenty years after the disastrous event, people forget about it, and wait for their own experience. In 1953 there was a general feeling that what had just happened must never happen again, and that the only way of having the maximum safety was to make a shorter line of defence, a shorter coastline, to close the estuaries rather than to heighten the existing dykes — for that is another possibility for increasing safety. If you have a delta or coastal zone where you have coastal maintenance, you can increase the safety by raising the embankments and being prepared for a higher storm surge, but that is not equivalent to an enclosure, because you then have two lines of defence, and in the case of a failure of the first line of defence you have still the second one. The probability of having a storm surge right after the first one is, of course, smaller than the probability of having the first storm surge.

Twenty years later people think differently. They talk about the significance of the eco-system and the brackish areas. They say, 'Why not increase the existing embankments rather than dam it off and produce a complete change in the eco-system?'

Of course economic factors play a role, for this type of work is very expensive and the difficulties are tremendous, increasing according to the nature of the area behind the estuaries where an enclosing dam has to be built. Whether such a solution would be feasible for an area like Bangladesh is another matter. This type of work was applied first in the Netherlands and Japan which could afford it and which have no other possibilities of storing water.

This does not answer the question completely, but perhaps it gives some philosophical thoughts on the factors behind the question.

Professor P. O. Wolf: In this country the situation is going to be changed, possible radically. I wonder whether Mr Beddoe could take this matter up in the context of legislation that is under consideration at the moment and the conditions as we find them, where in some cases minority groups with rather loud voices bring their influence to bear. I think there is a great deal of common ground in terms of conservation of resources in a gathering such as this.

Mr J. E. Beddoe: I am not quite sure what Professor Wolf wants. In this country we compare building reservoirs on the tidal flats and in the Wash, with water storage inland and upland. All I know is that whatever we do there will be a conflict of views. Whatever is proposed, if it means a substantial change in the local area, it will be controversial. We hope that the new organisation will enable the Regional Water Authorities, assisted by the National Water Council, to take a look at the whole system and find a balanced judgement, but whatever it is there will still be controversy.

Lord Zuckerman: Even after the Secretary of State has made his decision?

Mr J. E. Beddoe: Yes.

Lord Zuckerman: I do not think any decision taken about the environment today will be non-controversial until a new generation comes on the scene. Then the decision will be forgotten and new considerations will arise which will determine new priorities. Professor Volker talked about the eco-system. I am a biologist, but I may be the one person in this room who does not know what an eco-system is in the context of our discussion. I think I know what economics means. But Professor Volker left out a word — politics. I feel that because of the power of protest groups there would probably be the biggest international fuss if anybody were to suggest building the Suez Canal today, in spite of the marvellous opportunity it has given biologists to study marine biology in a highly dynamic state. The same goes for the Panama Canal. We are up against something which is, I hope, a transitory phenomenon in the issue of determining priorities.

I think that one thing which Professor Volker has really outlined and underlined is the realisation of how quickly people forget. I was in Norfolk when the 1953 disaster occurred. There were fears that the seas were going to break in again the day after. A year or two passed, and we were told that the county authorities were not going to give the money for the rebuilding of a certain coastal village which had suffered badly. A few years later the village was rebuilt. Has Professor Volker discovered how to persuade politicians in his country that if the chances of something happening again are, say, 5000 to 1, there is still the chance that it might happen on the following day?

Mr D. Ruxton: I should like to take up three points: first, the question raised by Professor Wolf about science; second, the damming off of inlets; and third, salinity control.

123

On the scientific question, so far as the development of models is concerned, we have only just reached the point where we can forecast surges against the coast when we make changes to the coast. In the past we have not been in a position to forecast what these new storm surge levels would be with new works. Similarly, difficulty has been experienced in representation of saline wedge movement after development. For the Ouse system, which is an extremely complex one, a model is now being developed which, hopefully, will describe adequately that system. Until 1969 this was not a real possibility. In Holland hydraulic models have been developed for small tidal ranges. This kept the sea surface at constant level and simulated the movement of the saline wedge in and out of the estuary. In this country the Thames mathematical model, developed for a large tidal range, moved the water surface up and down and the saline wedge was of constant thickness. We have now in the Hydraulic Research Station developed a model which simulates the sea surface movement and the saline wedge movement. Three different types of sediment are included and their transport in and out of the estuary is simulated. We hope this model will describe adequately the system. This model development has enabled the engineers to move away from the barrage approach for the Wash to the bunded reservoir approach, since judgements about the maintenance of navigation and land drainage can now be supported by detailed analyses.

On the damming of tidal inlets, I think that many engineers here were small boys, students or young engineers when the Zuider Zee was closed, so that all schemes for the storage of water in coastal areas have been coloured by this background. We have thought that a barrage is the better way to enclose tidal areas. We have been rather slow to withdraw from a barrage approach to a bunded reservoir enclosure approach. In the five schemes that have been considered in detail in this country recently, the only one that started with a barrage approach and seems likely to be developed that way is the Conway estuary. This estuary might be developed for recreational purposes. In the Dee and the Wash there has been a withdrawal from barrages to bunded reservoirs for the storage of water. On the Thames, tidal defence is needed and a barrier is to be built which can be raised against the North Sea surge. We are told, though we are not certain about this, that the final decision and the papers for this scheme were signed in Parliament on the day when the water level in the Thames was almost at the top of the wall outside the tea-room at the rear.

Lord Zuckerman: I cannot recall that piece of drama!

Mr J. E. Beddoe: It required a Private Bill and a great deal of other pressure as well.

Lord Zuckerman: It also required elementary lessons in probability.

Mr D. Ruxton: Turning to salinity control in the Wash, which is very close at hand, the problem has now been very largely avoided by the proposal for bunded reservoirs. Shipping would use the existing channels provided they could be maintained — and this is at present the subject of study — and so locking and intrusion through the rivers would not occur. The main problem here will be that of diffusion from the enclosed sea bed because the volumes of water we are dealing with from the Ouse catchment are so much smaller than those deriving from the Rhine catchment and the Meuse. We have reported already that flushing of the reservoir basins would have to take place yearly. Professor Volker said that 40 per cent of the total flow in Holland is used for salinity control. For bunded reservoirs this proportion of flow might be needed in the year of operation to flush out the enclosed area in order to get acceptable salinity.

Going on from there, if one brings Wash storage into commission slowly, the salinities in the water rise with the diffusion from the bed but if the storage is used to its maximum capacity immediately and there is a constant throughput, salinity is controlled well. This poses questions for future management of these resources, and if coastal reservoirs are not integrated with the other resources in the area it could be that water would become unpalatable. I say 'unpalatable' because it may remain drinkable. In Hong Kong, there was a water shortage when the Plover Cove scheme was brought into commission. The reservoir water level, though ultimately above sea level, was low at the time and there was sea-water intrusion through the spur of land between the sea and the reservoir. Water had to be taken from that reservoir to supply at salinities just over 1,000 ppm. This rather spoilt the tea and whisky, but people were able to drink it. With these coastal schemes this situation may have to be accepted on rare occasions. One of the objectives of the bunded reservoir proposals is to avoid it.

I would like now to turn to another aspect of salinity control. If the Wash scheme were brought into commission in a drought period, there would be a greater risk of having unpalatable saline water than if it were brought into commission in a period of large run-off. This is something that we might try to quantify so that we can justify spending the money early to avoid this. We could perhaps quote probabilities for a range of alternatives. As I read Professor Volker's paper last night it occurred to me that this was something we might be able to look into and quote facts and figures to economists who might make a judgement about whether it would be wise to put the storage in slightly early so as to be certain to reduce salinity in good time.

On the environmental issue there are two things I would say. The staged development approach is attractive because enclosure would take place by stages over a period giving least disruption. In the Dee, and probably also in the Wash, it is likely that the effect of the development proposed is little different from what would naturally happen with accretion, the areas enclosed for reservoirs being those that would ultimately have come into agricultural use. The Dee is an accreted estuary. Model studies show that the accretion has not finished, and of the areas proposed for reservoir development there are those that would become salt marshes. In the Wash, again, we have an accreting situation which seems to go in fits and starts; in some centuries accretion has been large, in some centuries small. This may be due to offshore sediments coming into the Wash entrance as a result of storms. From the entrance it would be reworked by the normal tidal system to form sand banks and raise the upper foreshore. These sudden changes in accretion rate can be partially explained by recent work by Professor Lamb about wind patterns and their changes over long periods of time. In any event, looking at the map of the area, one sees a steady accretion there and the bunded reservoir proposals now being considered are on areas which are already salt marshes and mud flats on the upper foreshore.

Professor A. Volker: I can only agree with what has just been said. In the first place, our scientific arsenal for considering schemes, for predicting changes and designing works, has been developed to a large extent, but there are still some important gaps. From the purely hydrological point of view of predicting the changes in tides and storm surges due to damming off certain parts which were formerly part of the tidal basins, I think the arsenal is sufficiently well developed. It is possible to have a physical model, it is possible to have a mathematical model, it is possible to have an electronic model to simulate the storm surges and predict changes in tidal amplitudes and ranges and storm surge elevation. What is very unsatisfactory is still the matter of sea water intrusion into open river estuaries especially when it comes to predicting the effect of dredging or deepening of the channels and the effect of adding tidal harbours to the systems. We still need a very intensive and very detailed collection of data on salinities which is not so easy, because the salinities vary with tides and the depths. They are different at different verticals of the profile. So there is quite a campaign necessary in order to collect the data which would enable one to predict how the salt intrusion will vary as a function of the fresh water discharge of a river. When it comes to predicting the effect of changes in the system itself, our arsenal of knowledge is still very deficient.

I am in agreement with what Mr Ruxton said about the alternative solutions of a barrage or bunded reservoir on the flats. This is again a matter of priority. The main priority is the defence against storm surges and, of course, a barrage type is the obvious solution. On the other hand, the bunded reservoirs are attractive from several points of view. They are much less expensive and do not require the difficult operation of closing the tidal basins. We have a number of those reservoirs on tidal flats on higher areas. So although the watertightness of such reservoirs can be a problem, it is certainly worthwhile to consider them as alternative solutions.

The matter of flushing or rinsing of the systems is one which may lead to conflict. Large amounts of water would be required. It is not so easy to convince the French and Germans about the necessity to consider the problem we have with the salinisation of the River Rhine. The same applies, of course, to the standard, the limit of salinity a river can have, because it would not be realistic to claim that the river water arriving from upstream should be absolutely fresh and have no higher salinities than 50 or 100 ppm. So we accept that the River Rhine is polluted. We depend very much on Germany and France in the Common Market so we have to accept some degree of pollution. I am thinking now of pollution by salt and not by toxic matter — that is quite a different thing on which there is also agreement. But what about the salinity? What are the tolerance limits? We have computed the mean average damage annually in Holland, in horticulture, and especially in greenhouses, as a function of the salt load of the River Rhine. We can compare that with the costs of retaining a part of the salt. That does not, of course, solve the problem of cost allocation. There is an agreement in principle that Holland pays 50 per cent of the additional costs, France 25 per cent, and Germany 25 per cent. That is at least a partial economic basis.

With regard to drinking water, the WHO has made recommendations with regard to the limit, but there is no harm in drinking water which is more saline. If sodium-chloride were the only contaminant in water one could, from the medical point of view, tolerate rather high limits.

On the question of the environment, what is the natural course of events? Certainly in tidal flats where accretion takes place the tendencies are to change from the marine environment into a continental environment, but the same applies to so many things that man is doing. Nature is doing the same, only at a much lower rate. Holland is blessed with natural gas. It has been predicted that a large part of Holland, because of the subsidence due to natural gas extraction, will settle in the course of twenty or thirty years by from 1 ft to 4 ft, which in the low-lying areas means something, because it is necessary to change the drainage system. It is a consolation for people to think that in 500 years nature will do the same thing, because we do subside now at the rate of about 8 in. a century.

Professor B. M. Funnell: I am impressed by the awareness expressed here of the problems which arise in the coastal zone on account of salinity problems, but how widespread is such knowledge? In a recent report on the Great Ouse pilot scheme, there is a suggestion to reduce the freshwater flow at Denver to zero, which would make the river downstream saline. Also I wonder whether in the plans for the transfer of fresh water into the Thames system the amounts involved are significant in terms of the balance between fresh water and salt water in the Thames estuary. It seems that at the moment the extent of incursion of saline water into the Thames is not a main concern. The first priority at present is to lower water levels to reduce flood problems; but will the introduction of larger amounts of fresh water affect water levels on the inside of the tidal sluices in the Thames London region?

Locally again it seems to me that drainage works in the Horsey Mere area are bringing in increasingly saline water from the sea because of the demand for drainage in that particular low-lying area, and we do not seem to be adopting a management programme which will keep saline water out. We also look for water supplies for coastal towns from well upstream in the fresh river water system (e.g. Wroxham) and thereby divert fresh water from the task of keeping saline water out of the river system.

How far are these conflicts, which Professor Volker has expressed clearly and Mr Ruxton seems to be much aware of in connection with the Wash scheme, generally appreciated in water management planning?

Sir Norman Rowntree: It is fortunate that the Government allowed these large wide-ranging feasibility studies to be carried out which have drawn on experience in Holland.

Due to the rate of technological development since the war, I think there was a good case for the environmental lobbies to warn the Government — 'Please be careful that you know what you are doing.' I think that warning is a good one. We did not often recognise these problems in the past, and we are indebted to Holland for having made the mistakes first and learned from them.

Lord Zuckerman: This is not the first time that this country has learned from Holland. Did not Dutch engineers have quite a lot to do with East Anglia many decades ago?

Professor A. Volker: We also have made many mistakes. The worst was precisely in the matter of the entrance to the Port of Rotterdam. Although we were aware of the repercussions of deepening a channel on the salt water intrusion, we were not sufficiently aware of what would happen (that may sound curious, because every engineer should know it) when one deepened the entrance to the estuary. Europort is located on the coast, Rotterdam is about thirty kilometres from the coast. Dredging was carried out in the North Sea and the channel and in the first part of the estuary. That deepening extended by retrogressive erosion further up-stream, so that the deepening of the channel up to Rotterdam was not caused by dredging but by retrogressive erosion starting at the mouth and then being propagated upwards. The only solution for reducing it was to throw sand into the river to make it shallow. The sand was then covered by gravel, in order to prevent the sediment from being eroded and carried back to the sea. That has now been carried out, shallowing and reducing the depths of those parts where navigation does not require those depths in order to reduce the salt water intrusion.

Mr D. Ruxton: On this matter I would like to say that we have these models, but very often it is the transfer of the information from the model to the full scale which is so very difficult. Let me cite two examples. One is the erosion of sediments in the sea and the other is the settlement of fine sediments. In the laboratory both of these were underestimated an order of magnitude. This is the difference between doing laboratory or model exercises and full scale tests, and that is why we engineers are pressing very hard to do some of these things at full scale – a small element of them at full size – before we get committed to the major work.

In regard to the change in the river to which Professor Funnell referred, there is a proposal in the Wash desk study that all the fresh water moving seaward that we are taking out should be replaced by salt water. This proposal was made after considering what might happen to the regime. Together with the Great Ouse River Authority we are making observations adjacent to the river. Tidal levels and salinities are being measured. We hope to assess the transmission speed of the water from the channels into the drainage system, and from these observations we shall judge the effect of this proposal to introduce sea water on the Fenland drainage systems adjacent to the channels.

As Sir Norman said earlier, it is the Government who have funded this, and we are able to do it. We will be able to give a judgement that is wide-ranging and which says not only what we can do about water, but what the effects of that will be on the present activities and on the other authorities with obligations and interests.

At the other end of the spectrum, in the Dee estuary, we had to consider how far the fresh water persisted seawards of the works so that the migratory fisheries could be maintained in that river. We were predicting penetration of fresh water rather than the reverse.

Mr B. R. Thorpe: We in Sussex, and in Lancashire it is the same, I gather, are under tremendous pressure to find additional sand and gravel from marine sources. Increased supplies are not forthcoming inland as easily as they used to be. Therefore there is additional stress on offshore dredging for sand and gravel. We are worried that there could be increased wave action as a result and that there could be a lack of beach replenishment on which the south coast relies for its defence against the sea. I should like to hear from Professor Volker whether there have been studies on this in the Netherlands. One thing that seems clear is that we have an almost total lack of knowledge of what the effects of marine gravel extraction are. We are constantly being asked to agree to additional extration resulting in the use of larger dredgers, and we are concerned at the absence of information on which to base our reactions.

Professor A. Volker: I am afraid I cannot give information on that point. The only thing I can tell you is that extraction of sand and gravel from the inland areas has become almost impossible. More and more sand and gravel is being extracted from the tidal areas and the offshore areas, but I do not know — apart from the repercussions on the channel I mentioned just now and the retrogressive erosion — of any cases where repercussions have been observed due to dredging.

Lord Zuckerman: This is a clash of interests which affects two Departments of State. But it is also a question of lack of knowledge. The direct clash has not focussed on coastal erosion, but on fisheries. At the moment, I believe, anybody can go outside territorial limits for his gravel. It would be extraordinarily interesting to know where the economic cross-over point was, so that in this country, for example, it would be more economic to remove the spoil heaps from china clay workings than dredge for gravel.

Mr D. Wilkes: The experience of Boston in getting sand and gravel to extend a runway at Logan airport is much like the problems which Britain may face for Maplin or other offshore structures. State authorities discovered that the Coastal Research Laboratory at the University of Massachusetts and the MIT sand transport specialists knew the general rules about the effects of removing offshore deposits; what they lacked was any primary data on current and bottom profiles for Massachusetts and Cape Cod bays which was detailed enough or prolonged enough to be useful. Their solution was to call a moratorium on permission to dredge up the sand while the Federal Government funded computerised field studies for MIT to get this data. It may not be rash to suggest that Britain may likewise need to involve its coastal universities in more intensive funded work to be able to rule intelligently on permits to remove offshore sand or gravel.

Lord Zuckerman: We have reached the end of this session, and I once again thank Professor Volker for his great kindness in coming at such short notice to lead this stimulating discussion.

7   Forms of Organisation

Mr R. C. CHILVER

It is dangerous to regard the similarity between electricity and water as a safe guide to organisational problems, but all the same it is worthwhile looking for a moment at the history of the organisation of electricity supply in this country. The key period was the late 1870s and early 1880s when technology had made it possible to use electricity on a large scale for lighting, traction and driving machinery. The immediate reaction of Parliament was to say, 'This is appalling. How can we prevent this ugly monster destroying our lives and emptying our pockets? Parliament then proceeded to pass a succession of Statutes which thwarted any attempt to rationalise the generation and distribution of electricity. Any operation by a private company was subject to veto by the local authority, which was quite often a supplier of gas, and even where it did not have that ulterior motive for being tiresome, it was apt to have ambitions of its own for generating electricity in due course. Those who put capital into electricity were told that within twenty years the local authority would have a right to expropriate them at cost. There was the famous Bermondsey clause, instituted at the insistence of a gas supplier, that the statutory undertaking must earn enough money by the end of its first six months to pay all its running expenses and start repaying its debt. Co-operation between neighbouring undertakings was positively forbidden – one could be sent to prison for talking to ones next-door generating company!

By 1930 there were in this country 650 generating stations. Besides ac at fifty cycles, dc or ac at nine other frequencies and a wide variety of voltages could be obtained. In some areas one undertaking could supply dc and another ac – with each undertaking having mains running under the same street. Between the wars the consumption of electricity per capita in this country was two-thirds of what it was in Germany and two-fifths of what it was in the USA. That was a fairly sad conclusion when one thinks that when the thing started this country possessed engineers who would stand comparison with the engineers in any other country in the world.

The effect on our economy of holding back the development of electricity is something that we are probably still feeling today.

I infer from that that we have got to be careful what we do about water, and we really cannot afford to indulge in aiming for constructive tension and elaborate checks and balances. I will not now go over the argument for unitary control of water activities, because they have all been set out and all of you have read about them.

It seems to me that the essence of the Government's proposals is to have strong Regional Water Authorities, self-reliant and with a feeling of responsibility. We must on no account do things which will force members of the Regional Water Authorities to sit back and say, 'We have our own ideas about how this show might be run, but the Minister, or someone, is preventing us all the time.' There is no reason why they should not feel wholly responsible for all things, including, of course, amenity.

As Mr Eldon Griffiths said, we have got to recognise that politics is the art of the practical. It was a tremendous achievement, when we look back on it, to have got through the Act of 1963 – one of the great socialist measures that we sometimes get from the Conservative party. It is not surprising that it got through a bit chipped here and there, above all in the excessive number of River Authorities, and that we have to amend it now; but still, I would judge it as in principle a more important measure than the one now before Parliament.

Going through the places where our present proposals have been attacked, one is leaving the company undertakings intact, though bringing them under the instructions of the RWAs. I think that is a pity. The task of treating water, whether you treat it before you put it into the river or after, seems to be a unitary one, as we all agreed when dealing with treatment. It is also a pity that part of the engineering and chemical expertise which is in short supply should be locked up in penny packets in these undertakings. Still, one cannot say that this is a grave blow to the Bill. It would be a very much more serious matter if it were proposed to give the municipal public water undertakings the same role as is being left for the private ones, because private companies are biddable, a local authority is not. Moreover, local authorities are responsible for control of development. The districts admittedly are not responsible for planning on a county scale, but applications for planning permission go to the districts, and it is not unjust to local government to say that one can visualise their response to a proposal from an RWA being influenced by their aspirations or considerations qua a public water undertaking. Fortunately, it does not look as if there is any grave danger of the municipal water undertakings being left in being like the private ones.

While I am not quite clear about the exact consequences of the provisions in the Bill for leaving some sewerage functions with the districts, it does look to me as if the essential features of unitary water control have been left intact. The districts qua sewerage authorities will in all important respects operate within limits laid down by the RWAs, and I do not think there will be any temptation for them to fall foul of the RWAs in connection with planning because of that sewerage function.

I think that one can say, looking back on past history, that it may be slightly unfortunate for the housing programme that this little bit of the RWAs job is being carved off and given to the districts, and again it is unfortunate to have these small packets of expert staff, but so long as it does not go any further than the Bill now says, there is no great harm in it.

The really essential thing is that the RWAs should control not only what is put into the rivers but what goes into the public sewers. It is far easier to prevent things like PCBs finding their way into the rivers if you intercept them at the factory gate rather than at the point of discharge into the river.

A third important modification is that, by contrast with what was said in the original White Paper, it is proposed that the membership of the RWA should be predominantly from local government. One can see why that may be an indispensable concession for getting the Bill through. One ought, however, to be clear about what it does and does not do. It does not give democracy, except in the broadest sense that decisions would be taken by men who were sufficiently interested in their fellow men to stand for local government and take enough pains to get elected. It is absurd to think that the voters in local government elections say, 'I am going to vote Conservative because I think they are much more inclined to be reasonable about the state of the Thames than the Labour people.' It is much more likely they will vote the way they do because of some quarrel about the Industrial Relations Act.

Again when a local authority nominates a member of an ad hoc body he ceases to be their representative. These people have been mentioned as representatives of local government, but the people we are thinking of are not representatives – they are nominees. I speak subject to correction, but from inquiries I have made I have always understood that the people who serve on ad hoc bodies like river authorities do not get a brief from the council. Nor are these local authority nominees a sort of appellate tribunal. Where protection of the individual is concerned, we have got to rely as in the past on the various rights of appeal to the Secretary of State, which the Bill is proposing to preserve intact throughout.

One more word on democracy. I do not think it is right to suppose that there is a complete absence of democracy in the appointment of members of an ad hoc body by a Minister. The Minister has been known not to renew the appointments of such people after the first three years. He has been known even to bring about their resignations before they have served their three years. He is much more likely to do that because they have been insensitive to public opinion than for any other reason.

I think that two major consequences flow from having a majority of local government members. One is that, unlike the nominees of the Minister, they will not be chosen because they have got something to contribute to the task in hand. They will be chosen because they are councillors and because they are not wanted for the housing committee, the finance committee or the general purposes committee of the authority on which they serve. I am not saying that they may not be able, but they are not chosen because they are peculiarly well suited to serve on an RWA. Another important consequence is that the size of the boards of the RWAs is considerably increased in consequence. I forget how many the Thames Authority will have, but it is of the order of fifty. The original concept of the board of a RWA was an executive body with a real meeting of minds round the table. There is all the difference in the world between that and a deliberative body where the chairman and perhaps one or two other members and the permanent officials produce proposals which are commented on by such of the other fifty-odd members as want to speak. One might argue that that is quite a good plan, that it is better from the point of view of the chairman and the engineer to have King Log and King Stork, but that is a cynical view.

One virtue that this proposal has is that it will help over the interface between town and country planning and water planning. If a councillor is a party to a decision to put forward a proposal that requires planning permission, he will feel some sort of obligation to support it when it comes to his council. He should not be regarded as a substitute for the contact that ought to take place between officials of the RWAs and officials of the local planning authorities, which is an essential way in which the RWA ought to ensure that it works within the county plan.

One other concession that has been made is that the number of water authorities has been brought up to a figure of ten. All one need say about this is that it gives quite a good pattern, but it would be pretty serious if one divided the country up even further. The key point here is that the bulk of decisions should be taken by the RWAs and not require consultation with another RWA and a joint project. I do not think that you will get the crispness and execution, the initiative and the drive, where there are two authorities co-operating under a plan evolved by the central planning unit that obtains where an RWA goes ahead on its own. It was of course, unfortunate that farmers insisted on thirty River Authorities instead of the fifteen that were proposed.

Finally, on organisation at the centre. The Bill provides for a clearing house for the ten RWAs in which they compare notes and arrange common services. I think that a great deal of help can be given to efficiency by comparing the practice in different RWAs. If an RWA thinks it is onto a good thing, it ought to tell the other RWAs about it, and consequently in due course it should be possible for the board of this body, the National Water Council, to evolve a system of efficiency not altogether different from the one that the British Railways board uses for effecting the efficiency of the different railway regions.

Another important piece of common service that the National Water Council can look after is standardisation of fittings. The price of plumbers fittings in this country is really shocking. If one goes to buy a piece of malleable iron or brass, one sees rows and rows of stock that the ironmonger has to keep.

In effect, the National Water Council will organise research and also information. The Bill proposes that there should be a separate entity which will take over the WPRL and so on and have a committee of its own, and be, as I understand it, a statutory non-profit-making company limited by guarantee. But the bulk of the members of the committee will come from the RWAs and the bulk of the money will come from them, and I see no great practical difference between having this research entity and giving the task of research to the RWAs. Either way provision must be made for the interest of Scotland and Wales and Northern Ireland, and the manufacturers have to be brought in.

An important part of the work of the National Water Council will be helping the Secretary of State to do his work. They will be the focus for contact between him and the water industry. So let us look at the Secretary of State's task. He has to decide what the total capital expenditure on water services should be. There must clearly be a rolling programme covering at least five years ahead, possibly five years in some detail and the ensuing five years in very broad outline. The Secretary of State is responsible for considering what is the appropriate figure, bearing in mind on the one hand the needs of the industry and on the other hand the limitations of the economy. He has also, in consultation with the National Water Council, to distribute that between the regions. He can not do his job properly if he merely says to the National Water Council, 'Here is £500 million in cash,' which they then divide between themselves. He must have some responsibility for the social consequences of the way in which the money is divided between one region and another or between the various components of water services, sewerage, public supply, and so on, he has got to distribute the capital expenditure.

He has also got all his present functions as to the protection of the individual against highhanded action by the water industry, notably over the compulsory acquisition of land. It would be a mistake to think that in exercising a function of that kind all that the Secretary of State has to do is send down an inspector, read the inspector's report and disagree or not. He must be supported by a staff which works out a philosophy which guides the Secretary of State's decision on individual cases. He can no more do without a staff on planning decisions about water than he can do without a planning staff for town and country planning. The inspector's job is not merely to think what is the right answer; that is, what the Almighty would regard as the right answer, or what he, the inspector, with his particular set of prejudices thinks is the right answer. He must give the answer that he thinks that the Secretary of State would give if the Secretary of State were doing the inquiry himself. So the Secretary of State must have a philosophy for the whole thing and he must have a staff to help him to do it.

Secondly, there must unquestionably be a staff at the centre to do the job of interregional planning which the WRB has been doing with such widely agreed success in the last eight or so years. I do not altogether understand the device that is described in the Blue Paper, under which this staff will apparently be in some way people from the Department of the Environment and, to quote the Blue Paper, will have an independent role; and as Mr Eldon Griffiths has told us that it would report to a committee which had a chairman appointed by the Secretary of State. I had hoped that the job of central planning could be joined with the traditional job of dealing with compulsory acquisitions, and so on, and that Sir Norman Rowntree, or someone of his stature, could be inside the department in charge of the whole thing. There are certain points of contact of a highly important kind between water planning at the national level and other kinds of physical planning. What is probably meant by having an independent role is that this planning unit should publish reports and should give its advice in public from time to time as the WRB has been doing. I am all for that. I do not see the need for a separate unit in order to have reports published. There is nothing to prevent the Secretary of State from publishing his own proposals on, so to speak, green paper to show that, like the proposals of the WRB, they are sub judice. However, there can be no grave harm in the central unit having an independent chairman and publishing its own reports, provided that for day-to-day working it is integrated with the Department. The greatest obstacle is that physically the people concerned are at present working in Reading, and in the present state of Government opinion about decentralisation of civil service staffs it would be a matter of the utmost difficulty to propose that staffs should be brought back from Reading to Whitehall. However, with the rather smaller range of planning work that will come to the centre because of the smaller of authorities in the field, the liaison between the central planning unit and the Secretary of State's direct staff should be tolerable.

There is clearly a danger that the Secretary of State will provide himself with a planning staff to advise him on the advice that he gets from the planning staff. With good sense all round that need not happen. It is not an essential part of the plan that the RWAs should not find a body interposed between themselves and the Minister. It would be inefficient, slow and disheartening for them.

We have got to recognise that Parliament is one tier of authority in this in a way that it is not over most government in this country: where water is concerned, Parliament takes its own decisions and sometimes rejects proposals by the Government.

If we have Parliament, the Secretary of State, the equivalent of the Water Resources Board and then the RWAs, we have four tiers. This is not the way that a dynamic thing like the management of water should operate.

At the moment we are in a very critical time. During the last fifteen years the basic situation has changed from one in which you got your raw water free to one in which you have to provide your raw water. We have had this great measure of nationalisation in the 1963 Act. We are now having a great tidying up of organisation. The ten men who will be the chairmen of the RWAs and the ten chief executives who will be the heads of their permanent staff will have a job to be envied. 'Blessed was it that day to be alive, but to be in the driving seat was very heaven'! I think that is the way we hope they will feel.

Discussion

Lord Zuckerman: We have now reached the point at which the discussion turns to the question of forms of organisation. This is a matter of Parliamentary debate at the moment. As Mr Eldon Griffiths reminded us, the Government, after several years of preparatory work, have put forward a Bill to certain parts of which it is totally commited. But obviously no Government can be certain about what may happen as a Bill becomes law. There may be pessure to introduce various amendments.

Mr Chilver's anonymity has already been exploded by the Minister, when he said that he and Mr Beddoe were part of the team which was responsible for the initial drafting of the Bill that is now before Parliament.

It is far more than an addendum that Mr Chilver has added to the statement that the Minister made yesterday. He has told us what the original concept was, and has reduced it to its base essentials. We appreciate why it is essential that the control of our water supply should be related to the control of what goes into our rivers. He has told us of the concept of regional authorities as self-reliant bodies, and he spoke of the reality of responsibility. I think we are all aware of the fact that the original concept was not totally translated into the print of either the Bill or the Blue Paper, and that there are some points which are still going to be disputed. Let us focus on them now. This obviously is a privileged occasion. No holds are barred and nothing is sacred.

Mr Beddoe may well be inspired to respond to points that are made and if he does he will be giving his own view and not committing anybody.

Mr J. E. Beddoe: I am still a hired mercenary. What the Government does is perfect!

Lord Zuckerman: May I begin by calling on Sir Norman Rowntree who has been at the heart of the problem for many years. He can give us the views of a body which is now about to be dissolved both because of the success of its efforts and as a result of the Government's decision.

Sir Norman Rowntree: May I say first that I am part of my time a civil servant, but fortunately I am also a member of the Board, and I speak now in the latter capacity. The Board is wholeheartedly behind the general principles of this legislation. It is imperative if this country is going to succeed and provide service in all aspects of water, that all aspects are brought together in the executive functions. The Regional Water Authorities should deal with all aspects of water use which interrelate.

Secondly, the Board agrees that the Board as at present constituted must go. The point of difference between us and the Government is what to put in its place.

May I continue in a more lighthearted manner. There is a peculiar astrological aspect about water. Graham Sutton, who was Director of the Meteorological Office until a few years ago, once said that droughts only seem to occur in odd-numbered years.

I would like to remind you of the drought of 1921, which was the worst we have had in modern times. There was the drought of 1929. There was the two-year drought which started in 1933, there was the dry spell of 1947, and there was the drought of 1949. There was a fairly dry spell in 1953, and a phenomenal one of 1959, which greatly facilitated the passage of the 1963 legislation. I draw your attention to two facts: one is that this is 1973, and the other is that the sun is still shining. I think –

and this is fairly serious — that if the dry spell continues, we could have quite a lot of problems this year. All I hope is that the general public does not blame them on the 1973 Act.

May I now be a little more serious. The 1963 Act had one remarkable effect, it suddenly set technology free, and many new concepts were developed. Ten years ago we would not have dreamed of the 1973 Act in its present terms. Everybody agrees to it in general; both political parties agree to the principles; the general public agrees. The reason the general public agrees is because it has been informed, and it has been informed by the Water Resources Board working with the River Authorities.

I think it may be appropriate to draw attention to the way in which the Water Resources Board as an agency has produced its reports. The work was done to a large extent by literally hundreds of committees of experts meeting many times. This work will now be crystallised in the next few months into one comparatively short report which will summarise the present situation through on England and Wales. It will be backed by a number of rather more complicated documents which will be of interest to the expert. I would emphasise that I suppose our chief function is not expertise but to see that that expertise already exists in the country is released. I would like you to look at the present Bill in that context.

We are told that the Board is being abolished because it was successful. I think it is being abolished because it is no longer necessary for the job it was set up to do. That does not mean that we do not need something like it for the next job.

The big advantage of the new legislation is the co-ordination of the dirty water side, and moreover, to contemplate the charging for clean and dirty water as a single charge. I don't know what the charging scheme is to be, but a good deal of the success of the RWAs and their public acceptability will depend on the way in which they devise a good, reasonably fair and simple charging scheme.

I am not happy that enough has been given to finance in the last few years. We are not as a Board equipped to do it, and I do not think the country, if I may be critical of the finance experts in the audience, is equipped to do it either. I have found it very difficult to find many people in water finance who could match up with the administrator, lawyer or technical person.

On the proposals for research we are unhappy. We think that one of the successes which we have achieved is the combination of a planning organisation with a body that is responsible for co-ordinating research and for seeing that it is done. The result is that money which the Government have been extremely generous in giving us has been devoted to things which are fairly certain to be useful. There have been very few exercises which have not to some degree been successful. I think we stopped three projects, but the third, desalination, was a major success, because by merely starting it we highlighted the enormous problems relating to that subject and reduced unneccessary expense.

In the future it is proposed to split planning and research. I think this has arisen because of confusion between research management and actually doing research. All that the WRB has done has been research management. It has ensured that the subjects chosen were correct, that money was available for doing them, and was given to the right people to do them. The Board would like to see the National Water Council have that research management function and be adequately staffed to do it, because as Mr Collinge has said on many occasions, you cannot administer research if you have not got people who know enough about the subject to talk to the experts. I think this research aspect and its splitting from the central planning function is a very serious matter.

We then come to the Central Water Planning Unit. Mr Chilver seemed a bit worried about its so-called independence, and that it is important that it should be directly linked with the Department. It highlights the difference between us. Mr Chilver genuinely believes that sort of function is primarily for the service of the Minister responsible and that he should have it readily available to him. My view is that it is more important that it should be seen to be an independent body, to which other agencies come openly and talk about projects before they go to the Minister with a crystallised opinion. I think that can facilitate Government decision and does not interfere with it.

The third problem at the centre is the interdepartmental problem. I referred to this in my Graham Clark Lecture last autumn, and I think there is no sign of that problem being resolved. The Department of the Environment has certainly taken the initiative in the past to get things done, and it is doing it on behalf of the Secretary of State for Wales. The Scottish Department pretends it does not want to belong, but now realises it has got to be involved in research and some other things. Northern Ireland have paid for the services of some of my staff in order to get the benefits from which they would otherwise have been excluded. The Ministry of Agriculture, Fisheries and Food is reponsible for land drainage, flood control and fresh water fisheries. Even the DTI is involved with desalination and the power generating industry, of which the latter represents about 60 per cent of the water used. We have therefore a big central Government liaison problem.

I repeat my wholehearted support for this legislation in principle. I congratulate everybody who has got this legislation into the programme.

Lord Zuckerman: We have heard Mr Chilver, who opened the discussion, deal with the genesis of the Bill, the principles behind it, and some of the changes which have taken place since he took his eyes off it. Now we have heard Sir Norman Rowntree, who has told us that at the very moment the Water Resources Board is about to disappear, there is a threat of drought.

Mr D. J. Kinnersley: I would like to pick up a very small point from Mr Chilver's remarks. He spoke of the Secretary of State's need to allocate the investment funds between Regional Water Authorities, and I wholly accept the need for the Secretary of State to do that, but Mr Chilver said that he would do it in consultation with the National Water Council, whereas the Department's party line, so to speak, has always been that this was one thing that the National Water Coucil would not be allowed to help the Department with. I must say that Mr Chilver's remarks that the National Water Council was to help the Department were very attractive, but they do give the impression, on occasion, of doing anything but actually arranging for the help to be given.

In the parts of the Bill that relate to pricing policy and tariffs, there are explicit references to the Councils being consulted on economics, but on planning one gets the impression that it is totally excluded. There is no reference to it in Clause 22, which is the planning clause.

There are two comments I would make. I think that the arguments advanced on the need for the planning to be in Marsham Street at the interface with town and country planning are all important, but people outside do not see them in that light. The water authorities will see them as an external authoritative element, as the alien arms of the Secretary of State and not as the collective activities of the water authorities themselves. If we had had the managerial authorities originally conceived we might have survived this, but now, with local authority dominated authorities, the need for the National Water Council to be seen as the collective agency of those authorities is very much more important. It is the need to make it be seen as such that the Department is still being grudging about, when in fact all the political pressure it is so quick to bow to in other quarters is in fact pressing the Department to do this. Like Sir Norman, I agree that the rest of the organisation is first-class.

Mr J. E. Beddoe: I should like to refer to both Sir Norman's and Mr Kinnersley's points. On investment, we are clear that discussions will be with the Regional Water Authorities, because, as Mr Chilver said, we want the Regional Water Authorities to be as strong and independent as possible. Equally, I think it is highly probable that there will be occasions when all

143

the RWAs will be dissatisfied with the total investment on offer. Then they would be bound to make their representations through the National Water Council.

Next, we are not so grudging as Mr Kinnersley says. There is an amendment to empower the council to advise on any matter relating to a national water policy, which covers planning. The Secretary of State has said that the Planning Unit will be controlled by a Committee which will have a majority of representatives of the National Water Council.

Sir Norman Rowntree raised the question of independence. What we mean by independence is that it shall be obvious and patent that the reports written by the Central Water Planning Unit are not tampered with by the Department or by anyone else. The reports will therefore be certified by the steering committee as being the work of the Central Water Planning Unit. We see a distinction between the reports of the Central Water Planning Unit and those which have been prepared by the Water Resources Board. We envisage the Unit producing the technical reports on the various possible strategies; but not, as does the Board, selecting from those possibilities a preferred choice. The National Water Council, the Department and other organisations will discuss the reports, making their own choice as to the best solution. Finally Ministers will have to select a strategy.

Whether this will work we cannot be sure, because there are difficult problems associated with very long term planning. We think it desirable that there should be discussion in the political arena of the various possible options so that when a decision is made it is conscious and deliberate. Until now when the Water Resources Board has produced a report Ministers have agreed that further investigation should be based upon the report but there has never been any long term commitment that this is really endorsed in a political forum. We hope the proposed machinery will ensure advice presented independently and a proper forum for political discussion; and that this may create, as far as is possible, general agreement on a broad, long term strategy.

On research, we envisage the Water Research Centre as being not simply a laboratory but also a research-commissioning body. The Centre will be responsible for the research at present commissioned by the Directorate General of Water Engineering as well as that by the Water Resources Board. The Centre will be linked with the National Water Council and the Department through membership of its steering committee. We hope to devise arrangements which will facilitate the flow of staff between the RWAs, the Council, the Department and the Centre. The Centre will bring together bodies which are separate at present and so create a much stronger and wider ranging research organisation.

Finally, on finance, I entirely agree with Sir Norman. This is one of the critical problems. One of the reasons for reorganisation is the need to secure integration in finance. At present sensible schemes founder because of the conflicting interests of the separate bodies affected by them. Conflicts which often reflect the way in which the incidence of cost will fall on different organisations, even though the scheme might be the best in its total effect on the community.

There is much to be done and there are difficult theoretical and practical problems to be solved. Work has begun by the Water Resources Board and some consultants on investment appraisal, and the Department has set up a committee to examine not solely investment appraisal but the complexities of an effective charging scheme: the proper allocation of costs between classes of consumers and the construction of a tariff which recognises these. Broadly speaking, we know the technical and scientific answers – enough of them – to know the way forward. We do not know the way forward on finance, tariff structures, and the like. I think that one of the most important functions of the National Water Council will be study and consultation on these subjects.

Mr G. W. Curtis: I should like to comment on Sir Norman Rowntree's remark that the public welcomes this Bill. Personally I do not think the public cares who supplies the water and looks after the drains so long as it is done properly. Much of the opposition arises personally from Members of Parliament.

I think the Bill is a brilliant concept. I think it will take a lot of bringing into effect. There are two stages one has to look at – the ultimate aim and the short term practicabilities of the Bill. Ultimately I would like to see in each RWA area a multi-disciplinary team. There is a vast increase in expertise involved, and this has repercussions. The major disciplines have got to be retained by RWAs either at the centre of each RWA or in one of the divisions possibly, which rather affects the cost of management units. I hope that the management units will not control the major expertise which ought to be available in the RWAs.

If I may touch on the point that I mentioned previously – the toxic waste disposal problem – this is basically at the moment with the county authorities. It is perfectly plain that county authorities will not have the expertise to handle this and the new RWAs will be intimately involved with it. Provided they have the expertise, they will have the control. We must concentrate the expertise at the centre of the particular RWA, or in not less than two divisions. I would like to see multi-purpose engineering teams which would create greater career prospects. The corollary of this is that we must alter the content of training for engineers in this country.

If you keep these controls at the centre or in the divisions of the RWA, you have then to operate them on the ground. This is the one big danger of the whole exercise. Those who are involved in construction work know the complications of getting an electricity supply when you want it in a hurry or of getting a few electricity poles moved. But it is no good prevaricating if the sewers are blocked — you must have an operational unit on the ground.

The problem in the short term seems to me to be a little different. The River Authorities are in the fortunate position that both they and the Water Authorities have undergone reorganisation within the last decade or so and have units which are capable of operating in their own right. This could carry on indefinitely until the RWA can get itself organised. So the Department has very wisely treated these as management units in their own right. In the long term the RWA will integrate these management units, and I think they should be integrated, but in the short term the River Authorities and the Water Authorities can carry on.

When one comes to sewerage and sewage disposal, one is in difficulties because this has not undergone the same reorganisation. The Ministry had it in its power to make sewerage boards, but there are very few in the country. What one has got is a hotchpotch of sewerage systems and authorities throughout the country, in the main operated by part-time people, who at the moment are undergoing local government reorganisation and whose main interest is going to be in local government reorganisation. Therefore, 'on the ground' there is not only a part-time organisation but an organisation which basically is not interested in sewerage.

The Department has formed these local management units for sewerage and sewage disposal on the same sort of thinking as it has applied for water and rivers; but, first, they are very much smaller, and, secondly, they have no personnel. When one looks at it, one finds that the major control of the sewerage and sewage disposal function, the design work, the policy work, the chemical work, must be done — because of this shortage of expertise — in a limited number of units within the RWA. The only function the management units can have is to keep the wheels turning.

I cannot see that there is any wisdom in having created these management units, which have an extremely limited and extremely short-term function until the RWA organises it properly and gets into its stride, and which cut right across local government boundaries. I do not argue for local government doing this, but the fact remains that for the next two or three years we have probably got to rely on the local government organisation to run these works. I do not like it, but there is no other answer. I

146

think it would have made the transition a lot simpler and easier if the management units had coincided with the new local government boundaries, either single units or a combination of units. The transitional problems are tremendous and I think it is on these transitional problems that a lot of the criticism will arise.

Lord Zuckerman: You are focusing our attention on some of the transitional problems?

Mr G. W. Curtis: Yes.

Mr J. E. Beddoe: Mr Curtis is right, but we are so far committed that we would cause more confusion by changing the basis of the units than by staying with them.

Mr D. A. D. Reeve: I agree with much of what Mr Curtis said, but I would like to look at it in a slightly different way. Mr Chilver, in terms of the Bill, of the removal of sewerage functions and allowing them to rest with the local authorities in a certain controlled way. I have no doubt at all that this will work, but there is a danger in doing this, because one of the big problems which an authority like mine has is in achieving a balance between the sewerage system, the collection system, and the treatment works — the disposal of it at the end. There is a very real risk of an imbalance between the two. This is a risk with the present proposals, but it is not an insurable risk. Having said that, I agree with Mr Chilver that this will work administratively. One has to look a little at the side-effects, and Mr Curtis has touched on them.

A side-effect is that sewage treatment has been divested at a stroke of all the management and administrative expertise that it really has in terms of these management units. These rest with the sewers and rivers departments, the sewerage departments of engineers and surveyors. These people have been excluded from the technical people who transfer to Regional Water Authorities through professional management units, and this is really extremely serious. However one is not demoralised about it; perhaps one should be, I do not know.

This having now been done, I think Mr Beddoe is right, and that one has to leave it and do what one can with it; but I think that the professional management unit working parties which have been set up, and which should have been operating for some time — some have not — are charged with the function of demonstrating their own shortcomings. I would hope that when these shortcomings become evident — and they will — it may well be that the department will have to recast its present proposals as to professional management units at the dirty water end.

Mr M. Nixon: I would like to stress one point about the administration of the RWAs. Sir Norman Rowntree referred to this in terms of government, where he had found problems of interdepartmentalism, and certainly the existing river units suffer from this very same ailment. Mr Curtis quite rightly said that the management of water resources is essentially multi-disciplinary, and I really know of no other system than the hydrological cycle where so many inter-disciplinary boundaries are crossed. So we need an inter-disciplinary approach to the management of water resources.

Unfortunately, as we are now to get between forty and fifty members in an RWA, this will perpetuate a committee system of management, and a committee system of management unfortunately rather favours the departmantalism from which we suffer at the moment. Somehow or other we have to avoid this happening if we are to manage our resources properly.

Mr R. J. Bell: I would like to comment on the question of corporate management, and say a few words about communications within an organisation with particular reference to the future administration of the RWAs.

There is no doubt that in the future the specialist must be absorbed into the multi-disciplinary corporate management team, in fact, the specialist must be on tap but not on top. It is very encouraging to see this is being accepted within the water industry but we still remember the great satisfaction when Sir Norman Rowntree was appointed as Director of the Water Resources Board, for he is an engineer.

We do not yet know the precise form of organisation that will be adopted for the RWAs but whatever is decided upon, communications with the organisation is a matter of great importance. I see an organisation as an effort to provide a systematic framework to ensure that communication occurs in the right form at the right time between those who need to communicate. As we move towards larger organisations I stress the need for good communications.

In referring to communications I am thinking of the written word and the spoken word. In may organisation, consultative staff committees are playing an increasing part, but communication in writing is equally important and here the use of jargon must be eliminated. The historian G. M. Young said that there were times when he felt civilisation would come to an end because no one would understand what anybody else was saying.

A well known member of the water industry has for a long time spoken about management for human happiness. I believe this is possible and I believe that in the water industry we are equipped to do this because we are used to dealing with people, not only members of staff but our consumers as well. On occasions, consumers ring me up at home and I also ensure that I am kept in touch with all consumer complaints. So I trust that the new organisations will not be so remote that consumers do not feel they are able to keep in touch with us who have the responsibility to supply wholesome water.

In conclusion, I think the times ahead are for optimists. I do not define an optimist as one who hopes for the best but one works for the best and is not prepared to accept defeat without actual trial.

Dr A. L. Downing: I should like to say three things about research. Sir Norman pointed to the need to link planning with research, and I think it is manifestly obvious that we shall continue to need some form of link. There must be dialogue between the planners and the researchers. The two functions have a good deal in common, and this is entirely consistent, if Mr Bell will forgive the jargon, with the present Rothschild customer-contractor relationship. Having said that, one must not forget that the planners are by no means customers of the research organisation. There is the whole spectrum of the needs for operating technology and the requirements of consultants and plant manufactures, who will presumably be paying members of this new Water Research Centre. They have to be catered for. So if what Sir Norman Rowntree had in mind was an exclusive link with the planning organisation, it does not seem to me that this would be right. One has to have the machinery for a close dialogue, and, as Mr Beddoe said, one way of helping to facilitate this is to have interchangeability of staff. I think that an exclusive connection with the planning function would not be in the best interests of the overall operation.

Secondly, on stability, I would plead for a period when we could have some stable future. Nobody on the research side wants to be insulated from the hurly-burly of political affairs. On the other hand, if you are going to do work which has got to evolve gradually over a period by painstaking effort on long-term problems, you do want some sort of stable background against which to work. In my own laboratory we have been under four masters since 1965 and now we are going to be under a fifth. I think this is really a bit too much. Eventually this kind of situation gets pretty demoralising. So I plead for some degree of stability when the final decision has been made.

Thirdly, I want to make a point about the role of the new Water Research Centre vis-à-vis the work of the RWAs themselves, in respect of what I think one should not really call their research function but their function of performing local investigations. It would be a great pity if a situation developed in which the RWA were beginning to set up large internal research empires of their own, because I think that in the end this would be to the detriment of the national interest. It would increase the fragmentation which one presumes the operation of the WRC is intended to avoid. So I feel that one must really think pretty carefully about the criteria that are to be used to judge whether a Regional Water Authority does local investigation or whether it should be more properly placed with the central unit.

Mr J. M. Boon: I should like to say straight away that I wholly disagree with Mr Chilver about the private companies. We are of course statutory water companies based on a very different concept from ordinary private enterprise. I think we have still something to offer. I hope that the Department will bear in mind that in the mobility of staff there is some expertise in the companies which might be useful in the general organisation.

Having said that, may I ask a question about the transitional period and the later period from a pollution point of view. I am chairman of the pollution committee of the East Suffolk and Norfolk Authority. Mr Eldon Griffiths put his seal on what our clerk, Mr Ellis, has been doing, namely, to say that if there has been bad pollution whether by industry or by local authorities, we have found it possible and indeed salutary to bring those concerned in front of the courts and, by example, to let others who do the same thing know what will happen to them.

Under the new concept of judge and jury, somebody in a RWA or Professional Management Unit might give standards of effluent or extend existing standards to a sewage disposal PMU of the same organisation, and I cannot see anybody in a RWA or a PMU prosecuting another unit of the same RWA. This worries me very much. There has been criticism of River Authorities that the local authority members have been loath to prosecute their colleagues in the local authority who run sewerage units. We have not found that in Norfolk. The prosecutions have had a good effect. I should like to know how this business of prosecution within the same organisation will take place.

I should like to comment on what Mr Bell said. I agree entirely with him about numbers. I have been very worried for a long time about the larger units. My company was a gas as well as a water company up to 1949 and the gas side is now part of the gas board. There were never strikes in the gas industry until it became large. We have never had them in the water industry. There is talk about one now. I believe all this has something to do with the larger units and the fact that a man does not know his immediate boss.

I am not happy about what Mr Bell said about engineers, although I am more than happy that Sir Norman Rowntree is an enginner. I am not certain that engineers are the right people to be the chief executives. Mr Chilver said this morning that the chairman would be nominated by the

Minister. Personally I think that the best administrator should be in charge, whether his discipline is engineering, law management, or anything else. I think this is wholly correct. I believe that the chief administrators of the RWAs should be men of any discipline so long as they are good administrators and managers. They can then sit back and not get tied up with a particular discipline, but can have the benefit of all the disciplines underneath them.

May I as a lay member conclude by saying how very much I have appreciated being allowed to come today and to join in this discussion.

Mr B. Rydz: I should like to say a few words on central organisation. We have established in our Board, I believe, some valuable and rather unusual links. The Board, which advises on policy, works closely with the team of planners – people who are analysing the relative merits of various strategies. And both are advised by groups of officers mainly concerned to establish priorities and to monitor progress in research and to provide specialised assistance to River Authorities in the field.

Mr Chilver suggested that it will be important for the National Water Council to review the alternatives put forward by the Planning Unit. This is something of a concession, perhaps, from where we stood at one time, but I think that this again understates the realities of the relationship. The planning staff of the Board have not been making propositions which appear out of the blue before the Board at one of its meetings. In our reports we have selected a small range of strategies from a vast number of options. This can only be done intelligently if there is a constant feedback of advice on what weight should be attached to certain propositions. I doubt if a planning unit within the Department can do a similar job and at the same time enjoy some independent status.

Mr Chilver gave us a picture of three or four tiers all involved in the whole field of endeavour. But I am thinking, not in terms of tiers of differing status, but in terms of a division of function. There is a lot to be said for dividing the country into regional units which to a large degree can manage their affairs, but in this country, because of our geography this leaves out of account important opportunities for the regions to help one another. It is for the water industry in its manifestation at the centre to evolve an integrated strategy and to keep some general, consistent lines of policy clear. This same industry, in its manifestation in the regions, will fill in the details of that framework. I suspect that if we do not have this, either the regions will not help one another to the degree that they should, or if they do so it will be done by quite wide-scale intervention by the Department.

Mr B. R. Thorpe: The third leg of what Mr Eldon Griffiths described as the central facilities was data processing, a small unit but nevertheless centrally organised. I would not wish to comment on the extent to which it is centralised, but what I do ask is that all of us who may be involved in Regional Water Authorities should have as an objective the introduction of compatible installations. It seems to me to be quite appalling that in the electricity industry they have taken almost a pride in having incompatible installations in each of their boards, and even when they have been compatible there has been further pride in developing programmes independently. There is a great deal of money spent on systems work and on programming, and it would be unfortunate if we did not achieve maximum benefit. ICL manufactures most of the equipment in the water industry, and it has the great advantage of being British. I think that we need to concentrate our activities in one firm so that we can develop compatible programmes and systems.

Mr V. K. Collinge: I should like to endorse what Mr Rydz has said about the evolution of the relationship between planning and research within our Board and to extend this a little further. There have been instances where the research side of the organisation has been engaged in the development of techniques and methods for the execution of the planning function and then has proceeded to hand these over, not in the way that one would have to do in separate organisations by the production of a long report and computer programmes, but by the physical transfer of the people who have done the job. This is by far the most effective way of moving research and development into application. There is no finer way of achieving this than by moving the people physically; and of course this has been a relatively simple operation because we have all been in the same organisation and very often in the same building.

Of course, in just the same way as the planning function has been carried out in very close association with the field agencies, so indeed has much of the work on which we have been engaged. Very many of our enterprises have been carried on a joint basis with River Authorities, with water undertakings, and in many cases with both. This is another way in which one can secure the advantages of central organised research and development facilities – the involvement of field agencies.

Our research and development capability has really developed in three ways. First, there has been a relatively small number of tasks but important ones, which have been carried out in-house for various reasons. At the other end of the spectrum we have contracted out many jobs more or less completely, and although these have been closely controlled, the execution has been external. But most of our projects have been between these two extremes, where we have been involved in co-operative enterprises. It is this spread of the method of execution of research and development which I think is responsible for much of our strength because we have had the expertise in-house — we have had the physicists, the electronic engineers, the mathematicians, the hydrologists, and so forth, who have been able to keep up with the subject because they have been doing research work themselves. Through this involvement they are able to stay in the forefront of their own technology. Yet we have been using those same people to control external contracts. I think there is no better way of doing this, because if we give a contract to a university, for example, and we watch it at regular intervals, we are watching in with a man who is in the forefront of that particular activity and he can tell when things are going to go wrong and can give some direction and purpose to that work if it needs it.

I think this has been a valuable feature of this form of executing research and development and I hope that it is the method of getting this type of work done which we will see incorporated in this new Water Resources Centre which we have heard about and which, of course, will have a much wider spread of activities.

Mr J. E. Beddoe: I should like to comment on some of the points raised by Mr Bell and others. One of the points which has been raised in different ways is the need to make the RWAs and their divisions multi-disciplinary. The management structure committee will recommend an organisation at RWA headquarters which compels a multi-disciplinary approach. Below headquarters the transfer from where we are now to the future must be made with the minimum disturbance in the field. Consequently a River Authority will become a river division and a water undertaking a water division in the RWA with very little alteration. For sewage disposal there is, as Mr Curtis said, the hard task of creating new units which will become divisions within the RWAs. There may well be a grave shortage of administrative, financial and in some cases professional support for the sewerage units. We hope that when we have the reports of the working parties, when we have identified the deficiencies, there will be some possibility of mutual help. Finally there will be a safety net; the power to use local authorities as agents for a limited time. The important job will be to keep all the services functioning and servicing the public.

In the longer run, I think the RWAs may wish to look at their structure and will not necessarily leave it in the present form. It may be desirable to integrate divisions as well as the centre instead of retaining divisions each responsible for one function. This cannot be done at once; the machine must be kept functioning. Reorganisation may continue after 1974 rather than at the date of transfer.

There is widespread agreement on the importance of delegation. The RWAs an not very large in number of employees – the largest may employ 15,000 people – but their areas are large. They will consequently have to take steps to ensure good communications internally, and also maintain touch with members of the public. We hope that there will be substantial delegation of authority from the RWA headquarters to the operating divisions. The management structure committee have already proposed and circulated a suggested delegation scheme which leaves a great deal of discretion with the man in the field. Dealing with the public, answering their complaints, giving information must, in the first instance, be for the local man.

Mr Boon spoke about prosecutions. The RWAs will be responsible for ensuring a supply of wholesome water, for maintaining and improving the river quality, and treating sewage properly. They will have responsibility for the whole cycle, and because of their duties, strong reasons for ensuring improvement at every point. There cannot be prosecutions internally, but certainly the divisional manager can be called to account.

Finally, the question of inter-RWA transfers. There will clearly be some inter-RWA transfers. Having said that, although these will be an important part of the RWAs' supplies they will be a limited part of each RWAs total supply and only a small part of their capital investment; nor will they be in the immediate future, the most difficult planning problems. The RWAs will start off with a framework which will have been created by the Water Resources Board's recommendations on national strategy which give the options and the choices for the major interregional transfers.

8 Summing Up

Lord ZUCKERMAN

Two simple propositions have underlain all our discussions. We have an essential and immediate problem, namely the provision of water for human and industrial consumption, and the provision of services to dispose of sewage. This is not a glamorous problem, and that perhaps is one reason why there probably are not enough skilled people in the country to fill places which will be created by the establishment of the new authorities.

Our second problem concerns tomorrow — that capital expenditure should be developed now for the continued well-being of the community. But, as we all know, the immediate problem is a worsening one, partly because, but only partly because, of population growth. A more important reason is that the standard of living is increasing everywhere. Dr Russell made the point that in the USA the problem of the redistribution of income has not been tackled in the way that it has been elsewhere, and that they therefore have to provide from Federal and State funds certain facilities — recreational and amenity facilities — which the people would not otherwise pay for. In this country the general standard of living is rising, and income is being redistributed. For example, in the part of north Norfolk where I live we have recently been provided with a public sewerage system. I have no idea who asked for public sewerage, but the moment we are all connected, people will have baths, there will be a greater demand for water, and greater costs will be entailed. Nobody can inhibit this process, because in our kind of democracy we keep looking over our shoulders to see how much better the other man is doing.

The growth of industry is another essential force in the demand for water. Developments in technology not only help industry alone but also make the problem of sewerage worse because of the dangers of added and sometimes new sources of pollution. But without more technology and more resources, we shall not be able to deal with this by-product of industrial advance. The problem of providing for tomorrow is obviously becoming more acute because of the increasing sensitivity of the public to environmental considerations.

To my mind there is no doubt that there has to be unitary responsibility for the water cycle. Those people who are responsible for extracting water have got to see that the sources they tap are kept as clean as possible. I do not believe that there is any disagreement with this concept. Put differently, the new Regional Water Authorities have got to be responsible for determining the right charge for their services, for getting people to pay for wholesome water, and for charging for the disposal of dirty water.

There is no precise definition of wholesome water, but we have standards and criteria it seems clear from this seminar that we do not have a good scientific basis for some of our criteria. Many clearly have to be arbitrary, since we cannot wait until we have all the facts before standards are set. Whether anybody can say that I am going to suffer because I have been drinking Norwich water these past two days I do not know; but I am sure that were I to drink 500 gallons of this today, I would be in hospital — not necessarily because of what chemicals the water contains, but for other reasons. Life is a risky business, and this is not a problem for practising doctors; they do not know very much about contaminants — they know about human beings.

A new body of expertise has to be developed which can advise about toxicology in a dispassionate and objective way, otherwise the problem of pollution will be dealt with mainly in terms of political pressures. We must find out more about the real risks, and we need to concern ourselves not just about cost-benefit — but about risk-benefit, a concept which receives far too little attention. To what extent are the risks of doing something offset by the benefits? When one is really parched one will drink any water.

In our opening session Mr Rydz told us what the balance-sheet shows for the future. He provided figures, and they are the best figures we have. We have also been shown what the problem is in the Netherlands. The immediate one is the provision of water, the prevention of pollution, the prevention of salt intrusion, and so on. And we have discussed various ways in which these things can be done.

These are all matters which affect us today. But it has also become obvious that unless we know how to direct our actions today, we shall have worse problems tomorrow. When Professor Volker told us that the extraction of gas in the Netherlands is making the land sink slightly faster than it would otherwise, I wondered whether anybody had done the necessary sums to equate the energy value of the gas extracted to the amount of energy which might be necessary to lift the land surface in order to prevent flooding by the sea.

There is another set of potential problems which are important. They were dealt with very well by Mr Thorpe. There is the essential need to prevent the spoliation of the land. Although there is no common view, one certainly knows what the bulk of the people would want in the way of amenities. I do not know whether the conflict between canoeists and

156

anglers could ever be resolved; that is a matter for politicians and the judiciary.

But what does matter to an academic audience is the emotional attitude of the new school of non-academically and non-scientifically trained ecologists. I have not doubt that had they been around to express a view about the cutting of the Suez Canal, they would have said 'no'. Had they been asked to decide whether or not the Fens should be drained, they would have said 'no'. That kind of emotional attitude to the environmental problem can become a vested and undemocratic interest opposed to the interests of the majority. Our problems certainly contain an element of the irrational.

As Mr Chilver, Mr Beddoe and indeed Mr Eldon Griffiths have indicated, in the end the issues boil down to questions of politics and economics. Somebody has got to decide what is best. A succession of Acts of Parliament have been designed in order to protect the public and the environment. We have this present Bill. As this discussion has indicated, it might have been a better Bill but it is unlikely to be the last in the series! We are passing through a transitional period, and I hope very much that the new authorities will realise that they have got to spend their first five years designing their administrative structures even better than the Act spells out. Sir Norman Rowntree indicated only too clearly that he is not satisfied by what is being proposed for research and development.

But let us take heart. I am an optimist. As Sir Frederick Warner said, however many unknowns there are in this field, it remaines more predictable than others, more predictable than the future of an industry, for instance, with no more than an average five years for any prevailing technology. Moreover, there is no sense of doom about the problems with which we have been dealing. The taps are never turned off, the plugs still work, whereas trains and buses often do not run. If only the same kind of awareness were abroad about matters like public and private transport as about the problem of the water cycle, then the jobs of our political masters would be easier than they are now. What problems there are about water and sewage are in part a challenge to the universities. Their solution can be based upon the sophisticated application of knowledge which exists and of knowledge which we know will be gained. For the future we need trained personnel from many disciplines. For the past we can be grateful to the work that has been done by the authorities which were set up by previous Acts of Parliament, by the Water Resources Board, by the River Authorities, and by the sewerage authorities. They have all helped provide the knowledge on the basis of which the new Bill has been designed.

Appendix

List of official reports and legislation relating to water management in England, Wales and Scotland, published since 1945

compiled by K. V. Bowles, Librarian, Water Research Association

SECTION 1 – OFFICIAL REPORTS

England and Wales

Health, Ministry Agriculture and Fisheries, Ministry, and Scotland, Health Department. A national water policy (London, HMSO, Cmnd 6515, 1944).

Health, Ministry: Committee on causes of increase in consumption of water. Interim report (London, HMSO, 1949).

Housing and Local Government, Ministry Central Advisory Water Committee. Sub-Committee on the Growing Demand for Water. Reports (1st, 2nd and final) (London, HMSO, 1959–62).

Housing and Local Government, Ministry and Welsh Office. Taken for granted; report of the working party on sewage disposal (London, HMSO, 1970).

Environment, Department. Reorganisation of water and sewage services: government proposals and arrangements for consultation (London, HMSO, 1971).

Environment, Department: Central Advisory Water Committee. The future management of water in England and Wales (London, HMSO, 1971).

Environment, Department and Welsh Office: Working Party on Sewage Disposal. Report (London, HMSO, 1972).

Environment, Department, and Welsh Office. Background to water reorganisation in England and Wales (London, HMSO, 1973).

Scotland

Scottish Development Department: Scottish Water Advisory Committee. The water service in Scotland (Edinburgh, HMSO, 1972).

Scottish Development Department: Scottish Water Advisory Committee.

Final Report – the water service in Scotland (Edinburgh, HMSO, Cmnd 3116, 1966).

Scottish Development Department: Scottish Water Advisory Committee. 3rd Report – the water service in Renfrewshire (Edinburgh, HMSO, 1964).

Scottish Development Department: Scottish Water Advisory Committee. 2nd Report – the water service in Ayrshire (Edinburgh, HMSO, 1964).

Scottish Development Department. Scottish Water Advisory Committee. 1st Report – the water service in Central Scotland (Edinburgh, HMSO, 1963).

Scottish Development Department. A measure of plenty; water resources in Scotland – a general survey (Edinburgh, HMSO, 1973).

SECTION 2 – LEGISLATION

England and Wales

Water Act, 1945 (London, HMSO, 1945).
Rivers (Prevention of Pollution) Act, 1951 (London, HMSO, 1951).
Water Act, 1958 (London, HMSO, 1958).
Clean Rivers (Estuaries and Tidal Waters) Act, 1960 (London, HMSO, 1960).
Rivers (Prevention of Pollution) Act, 1961 (London, HMSO, 1961).
Water Resources Act, 1963 (London, HMSO, 1963).
Rural Water Supplies and Sewerage Act, 1965 (London, HMSO, 1965).
Rural Water Supplies and Sewerage Act, 1971 (London, HMSO, 1971).
Water Resources Act, 1971 (London, HMSO, 1971).
Water Act, 1973 (London, HMSO, 1973).

Scotland

Rivers (Prevention of Pollution) (Scotland) Act, 1951 (London, HMSO, 1951).
Water (Scotland) Act, 1967 (London, HMSO, 1967).
Rivers (Prevention of Pollution) (Scotland) Act, 1965 (London, HMSO, 1965).
Rural Water Supplies and Sewerage (Scotland) Act, 1969 (London, HMSO, 1969).

List of Participants

Professor Lord Zuckerman, OM, KCB, FRS

Dr R. G. Allen, Water Research Association
Mr P. L. Ashford, East Suffolk and Norfolk River Authority
Mr M. Baldwin, School of Environmental Sciences
Mr J. E. Beddoe, Department of the Environment
Mr R. J. Bell, Norwich Water Department
Mr J. M. Boon, East Anglian Water Company
Dr G. S. Boulton, School of Environmental Sciences
Mr R. C. Chilver, formerly Department of the Environment
Dr B. G. Clarke, School of Environmental Sciences
Mr K. B. Clarke, East Anglian Water Company
Prof. K. M. Clayton, School of Environmental Sciences
Mr V. K. Collinge, Water Resources Board
Mr G. W. Curtis, Norfolk Public Health Engineering Department
Dr A. L. Downing, Water Pollution Research Laboratory
Mr S. V. Ellis, East Suffolk and Norfolk River Authority
Prof. B. M. Funnell, School of Environmental Sciences
Mr Eldon Griffiths, Department of the Environment
Dr J. G. Harvey, School of Environmental Sciences
Dr R. D. Hey, School of Environmental Sciences
Mr D. J. Kinnersley, Association of River Authorities
Prof. H. H. Lamb, Climatic Research Unit
Dr P. S. Liss, School of Environmental Sciences
Mr J. McLoughlin, University of Manchester
Mr M. Nixon, Trent River Authority (Deceased 21/2/74)
Dr J. Rees, London School of Economics and Political Science
Mr D. A. D. Reeve, Upper Tame Main Drainage Authority
Mr H. Richards, Water Resources Board
Sir Norman Rowntree, Water Resources Board
Dr C. Russell, Resources for the Future, Washington, USA
Mr D. Ruxton, Binnie and Partners, Consulting Engineers
Mr B. Rydz, Water Resources Board
Dr M. E. C. Sant, Centre of East Anglian Studies
Dr K. Smith, University of Strathcylde

Mr B. R. Thorpe, Sussex River Authority
Mr P. M. Townroe, Centre of East Anglian Studies
Mr H. van Oosterom, Great Ouse River Authority
Sir Frederick Warner, Cremer and Warner, Consulting Engineers
Dr P. Warren, Cabinet Office
Mr D. Wilkes, Water Resources Center, University of Massachusetts
Prof. P. O. Wolf, City University